Advanced Mathematics

Precalculus with Discrete Mathematics and Data Analysis

Activities Book

McDougal Littell/Houghton Mifflin

Evanston, Illinois

Boston   Dallas   Phoenix

About the Activities

The activities in this book range from applications, such as *Contour Maps*, to enrichment, such as *Comparing Residuals*, to creative problem solving, such as *Assessing Risk*. Their subject matter should appeal to a wide range of student interests. Historical references are made when appropriate, and the activities *Finite Differences*, *Equation Solving in Ancient Civilizations*, *History of Trigonometry*, and *Mathematicians of Alexandria* highlight the multicultural origins of mathematics.

Acknowledgements

The following teachers and mathematics supervisors have written activities for this book.

Dane Camp
Mathematics Teacher
Downer's Grove South High School
Downer's Grove, Illinois

Robert Cornell
Mathematics Department Chairperson
Milton Academy
Milton, Massachusetts

James J. Landherr
Mathematics Coordinator
East Hartford Public Schools
East Hartford, Connecticut

Dorothy Peterson
Mathematics Department Chairperson
Jefferson High School
Cedar Rapids, Iowa

Loring Coes III
Mathematics Chairperson
Rocky Hill School
East Greenwich, Rhode Island

Donna DiFranco
Professor of Mathematics
Bentley College
Waltham, Massachusetts

Lois Martin
Mathematics Teacher
Downingtown High School
Downingtown, Pennsylvania

Joan Piper
Mathematics writer and editor, formerly
Mathematics Department Chairperson
Milton Academy
Milton, Massachusetts

ISBN-13: 978-0-395-52926-3   ISBN-10: 0-395-52926-3

9 10 11 12-CSM-08 07

Contents

Using the Activities

Introduction

The twenty-four activities in this book can be used in a variety of different ways to involve students actively in learning advanced mathematics. Although the activities vary widely in content, they all provide opportunities to develop students' abilities to solve problems, to discuss mathematical ideas, to reason about concepts and think critically, and to look for and make connections among different parts of mathematics and real-world situations.

How Can I Use These Activities in My Class?

Essentially, there are two basic ways that these activities can be used in class—for group work or for individual work. In either case, the activities can be used to encourage student participation in the learning process. The following paragraphs discuss briefly how this can be done. First, let's take a look at the use of cooperative learning groups as a means of using the activities in class.

What is a Cooperative Learning Group?

Put simply, a cooperative learning group is two or more students working together on a common task. To keep the work of the group manageable and focused, it is usually recommended that groups have from three to five students in them. The activities in this book provide specific tasks for group work. In addition to having students work in groups in class, you might consider having groups work on some of the activities outside of class. These groups should be small, perhaps only two or three students, and they should be required to present their results to the entire class.

What Do Students Learn in Groups?

One of the major benefits of small group work is creating an environment in which students can learn to do mathematics together, discuss ideas, pool problem-solving resources, and communicate their results to others. Groups help to engage students actively in learning mathematics, and in so doing, can transform the mathematics classroom into a more dynamic and enjoyable place of learning. As students work in groups, they also learn to work together with others to solve common problems.

Group activities should be focused on solving problems, discussion, thinking together, making connections, and presenting results. All students need to be encouraged to participate in these aspects of group work. The ACTIVITIES BOOK provides materials that you can use to incorporate cooperative learning groups into your classroom.

Using Physical Models

The use of physical models is entirely appropriate in teaching and learning advanced mathematics. Whenever possible, encourage students to make models to explain their ideas. Models help students to understand abstract concepts and to develop sound intuitions that support future learning.

Individual Work

At times, you may wish to assign some of the activities to individual students for work outside of class. These assignments can be treated as special projects or investigations. If the activities are used in this way, it is important to consider some follow-up. For example, students can give brief verbal reports to the class on their individual projects, explaining the activity and what they have learned by doing it. These kinds of presentations help to develop communication skills and enrich the backgrounds of other students in the class.

Any one of the activities in this book can also be used as a basis for a more extended research report by a student. Such a report can be written and included in a student's portfolio, if one is being developed. At this level of studying mathematics, students need to begin to learn how to work more independently. All reports, whether written or verbal, should be evaluated. Written comments rather than a numerical grade would be more helpful to students in understanding their performance on any particular project. Comments should relate to problem solving, critical thinking skills, and communication skills, and be focused on growth in understanding mathematical ideas rather than on manipulative skills and algorithmic ways of thinking.

NAME _____   DATE _____

Using Parabolas to Solve Quadratic Equations
(For use with Section 1-7)

As noted in Section 1-7, the *x*-intercepts of the parabola

$$y = ax^2 + bx + c$$

are the real roots of the quadratic equation

$$ax^2 + bx + c = 0.$$

In the following activity, you will draw a few basic parabolas and use them to find the real roots of related quadratic equations.

Activity: Translating Parabolas and Finding x-intercepts

For this activity you will need a sheet of quarter-inch graph paper, a sheet of transparent film (commonly called a "transparency" when used on an overhead projector), a pencil, and a marker made for writing on the transparency.

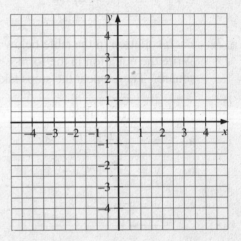

As shown at the right, draw a set of axes in the middle of the graph paper, and label the axes so that one-half inch equals one unit. Place a corner of the transparency over the axes on the graph paper, and use the coordinate grid to draw an accurate graph of $y = x^2$ for $-3 \le x \le 3$. Show the parabola's vertex and axis of symmetry, and label the parabola with its equation. Then, in two other corners of the transparency, do the same for the parabolas $y = 2x^2$ and $y = \frac{1}{2}x^2$.

You can now use the "basic" parabolas that you have drawn to obtain the graphs of other quadratic equations. For example, to obtain the graph of $y = (x - 3)^2 + 1$, you would position the basic parabola $y = x^2$ over the coordinate grid on the graph paper so that the vertex of the parabola is at the point $(3, 1)$, the axis of symmetry is parallel to the *y*-axis, and the parabola opens upward. In effect, you have *translated*, or shifted, each point on the basic parabola 3 units to the right and 1 unit up, as shown at the right. (You will learn more about translating graphs in Chapter 4.)

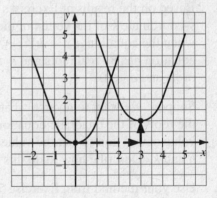

1. Describe how to obtain the graph of $y = -(x - 3)^2 + 1$ from the graph of $y = x^2$.

In Exercise 1, *two* geometric transformations are required to obtain the graph of $y = -(x - 3)^2 + 1$ from the graph of $y = x^2$. Before translating the basic parabola, you must *reflect* it in the *x*-axis (that is, flip it over the *x*-axis) so that the parabola opens downward. (You will learn more about reflecting graphs in Chapter 4, too.)

ADVANCED MATHEMATICS
Activities Book

NAME _____ DATE _____

Using Parabolas to Solve Quadratic Equations *(Continued)*

2. Each equation in the table below has the form $y = a(x - h)^2 + k$. From the equation, determine the coordinates of the vertex of the equation's graph. Then use the basic parabola $y = ax^2$ to obtain the equation's graph. Finally, determine the x-intercepts of the graph to find the real roots of the equation $a(x - h)^2 + k = 0$ (that is, the value(s) of x for which $y = 0$ in the equation $y = a(x - h)^2 + k$).

	Equation	Vertex of graph	Real roots when $y = 0$
a.	$y = (x - 1)^2 - 9$	?	?
b.	$y = -2(x + 3)^2 + 2$	?	?
c.	$y = \frac{1}{2}(x + 4)^2 + 2$	?	?

3. Each equation in the table below has the form $y = ax^2 + bx + c$. Write the equation in the form $y = a(x - h)^2 + k$ by completing the square. Then repeat the steps taken in Exercise 2.

	Equation	Vertex of graph	Real roots when $y = 0$
a.	$y = -x^2 + 4x - 4$	?	?
b.	$y = 2x^2 + 2x - 4$	?	?
c.	$y = -\frac{1}{2}x^2 + x - 3$	?	?

4. Based on the results of Exercises 2 and 3, what can you say about the y-coordinate k of the vertex of the graph of $y = a(x - h)^2 + k$ when the equation $a(x - h)^2 + k = 0$ has a *double* root? when the equation has *no* real roots and $a > 0$? when the equation has *no* real roots and $a < 0$?

5. Suppose we want to reverse what we've been doing. That is, given the roots of the quadratic equation $a(x - h)^2 + k = 0$ where the value of a is known but the values of h and k are not, we want to find h and k. Describe how to do this using the basic parabola $y = ax^2$.

6. Use your method from Exercise 5 to complete the table below.

	Roots	Vertex of $y = a(x - h)^2 + k$ when $a = 1$	when $a = 2$	when $a = -\frac{1}{2}$
a.	$x = 1, x = 3$	?	?	?
b.	$x = -2, x = 4$	?	?	?
c.	$x = 3, x = -1$	?	?	?

ADVANCED MATHEMATICS
Activities Book

NAME _____   DATE _____

Algorithms and Polynomial Time
(For use with Section 2-1)

Efficient Algorithms

At the heart of computer science is the search for a clear and precise procedure for solving a given problem. Such a procedure is called an *algorithm*, which is a Latinized version of the name of the ninth-century Arab mathematician al-Khowarizmi.

   In Section 2-1 you were introduced to the synthetic substitution algorithm. As the Computer Exercises on page 58 of the text show, this algorithm is more *efficient* than other methods of evaluating polynomials because it involves fewer operations (and therefore takes less time).

   To get a better idea of what it means for one algorithm to be more efficient than another, consider the two given below. Both are procedures for finding the greatest common factor (GCF) of two positive integers.

Trial Divisions Algorithm

   1.   Accept two positive integers M and N (with $M > N$).
   2.   Set D equal to 2, and set F equal to 1.
   3.   Repeat the following until $D > N$:
       a. Set $Q1$ equal to M divided by D, and set $Q2$ equal to N divided by D.
       b. If both $Q1$ and $Q2$ are whole numbers, then set F equal to the product of F and D, replace M with $Q1$, replace N with $Q2$, and go back to (3).
       c. If either $Q1$ or $Q2$ is *not* a whole number, then increase D by 1 and go back to (3).
   4.   Report that the greatest common factor is F.

Euclidean Algorithm

   1.   Accept two positive integers M and N (with $M > N$).
   2.   **a.** Set Q equal to the integer part of M divided by N, and set R equal to the difference between M and the product of Q and N.
       b. If R is *not* 0, then replace M with N, replace N with R, and go back to (a).
   3.   Report that the greatest common factor is N.

---

1. **a.** Do a trace of each algorithm by making a list of all the variables involved and keeping track of each variable's current value (by crossing out old values and writing down new ones) as you carry out the steps of the algorithm. For each trace, let $M = 36$ and $N = 24$ (that is, use each algorithm to find the GCF of 36 and 24). The trace of the Euclidean algorithm is started at the right.

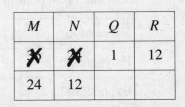

M	N	Q	R
~~36~~	~~24~~	1	12
24	12		

    b. A good indicator of the efficiency of each algorithm is the number of divisions that must be performed. Using the traces of part (a), determine which algorithm is more efficient.

ADVANCED MATHEMATICS
Activities Book

Algorithms and Polynomial Time (Continued)

2. To confirm your answer to part (b) of Exercise 1, write computer programs to implement the two algorithms. Then, using large numbers for M and N, run each program to see which one takes longer to execute.

Since the efficiency of an algorithm can vary depending on the data used, computer scientists often consider the worst case. For the Euclidean algorithm, the worst case occurs when N divides M exactly once each time step 2(a) is performed.

3. **a.** Confirm that the worst case occurs when using the Euclidean algorithm to find the GCF of 89 and 55. How many divisions are performed?

   b. Try to find another pair of two-digit numbers that result in the worst case for the Euclidean algorithm.

4. What is the worst case for the trial divisions algorithm? Give an example using a pair of two-digit numbers.

Polynomial Time versus Exponential Time

As the size of a problem grows, the efficiency of an algorithm for solving the problem becomes increasingly important. Therefore, for a problem of size n, computer scientists are interested in determining a function of n that roughly gives the number of computations needed to solve the problem using a particular algorithm. For example, in the case of finding the GCF of two positive integers, if we define n as the number of digits in the larger integer, then we find that the Euclidean algorithm requires about $5n$ divisions in the worst case. Because $5n$ is a polynomial, we say that the Euclidean algorithm runs in "polynomial time." The trial divisions algorithm, on the other hand, runs in "exponential time."

5. Both polynomial and exponential functions involve powers. For a polynomial function, the base is a variable and the exponent is a constant; for an exponential function, the base is a constant and the exponent is a variable. To appreciate this distinction, copy and complete the table below. (Use the power key on a calculator to obtain the values of the exponential function. You will learn more about such functions in Chapter 5.)

Value of n	1	2	3	4	5	...	10	...	50	...	100
Polynomial: n^2	?	?	?	?	?	...	?	...	?	...	?
Exponential: 2^n	?	?	?	?	?	...	?	...	?	...	?

6. Use Exercise 5 to compare the "behavior" of polynomial functions of n and exponential functions of n when **(a)** the value of n is small and **(b)** the value of n is large.

Algorithms and Polynomial Time (Continued)

Unfortunately, there are many important problems for which the obvious algorithm that solves the problem runs in exponential time. A classic example is the traveling salesman problem, where a salesman who must visit each of n cities wants to minimize the total distance to be traveled (see pages 824 and 825 of the text). If *all* possible routes are checked in order to find the shortest one, the procedure can take *years* of computer time even when the number of cities is only 20 or so. Fortunately, the nearest-neighbor algorithm (in which a route is chosen by moving from one city to whatever unvisited city is closest) runs in polynomial time and finds a route that may not be the shortest, but is shorter than most.

As our discussion of the traveling salesman problem has shown, computer scientists must often settle for algorithms that give an *adequate* (if not the best) solution to a problem in a *reasonable* amount of time.

7. Consider the bin-packing problem: Suppose you want to put packages of various sizes into bins of fixed size. How are you to arrange the packages so that the minimum number of bins is used?

    a. Shown at the right is one way to arrange packages of length 7, 6, 6, 4, 3, 3, 3, 2, and 2 in four bins of length 12. Rearrange the packages so that they fit into only three bins of length 12.

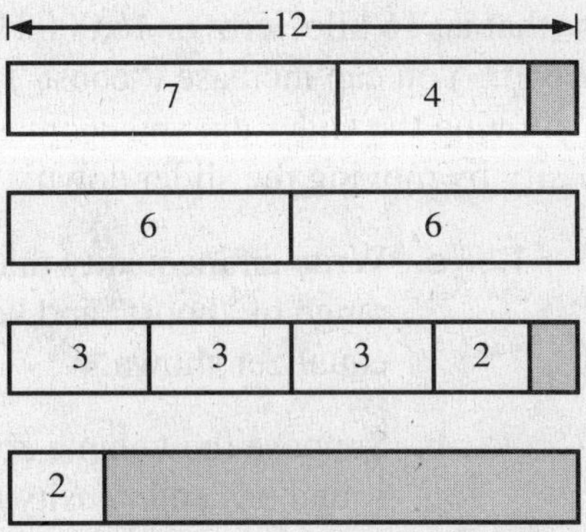

    b. An algorithm that checks all possible arrangements of packages in order to determine which arrangement requires the least number of bins runs in exponential time. The first-fit algorithm, however, runs in polynomial time. This algorithm takes each package, in order of decreasing size, and places it in the first bin that can accommodate it. Use the first-fit algorithm with bins of length 10 and packages of length 6, 5, 4, 4, 3, 3, 3, and 2.

    c. In part (b), can you find a better fit than the first-fit algorithm gives?

ADVANCED MATHEMATICS
Activities Book

Equalizers and Inequalities
(For use with Section 3-1)

An equalizer is a popular accessory component for a stereo system. It allows you to control the sounds output by a stereo by altering the intensity of various bands of frequencies. A sound's *intensity* determines the sound's perceived *loudness* and is measured in decibels (dB). A sound's *frequency* determines the sound's perceived *pitch* and is measured in vibrations per second, or hertz (Hz). A greater frequency produces a higher pitch.

A typical ten-band equalizer is shown at the right. Each slider controls a range of frequencies and is identified by a central frequency of the band, from 32 Hz on the low end to 16 kHz (that is, 16 kiloHertz or 16,000 Hz) on the high end. You can increase ("boost") intensity by moving the slider up, and decrease ("cut") intensity by moving the slider down.

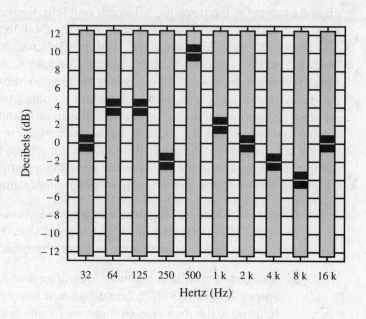

1. **a.** Write an inequality that expresses, for any frequency band, the range of "boost" and "cut" in intensity that is possible with the equalizer shown.

    b. Suppose the volume control of a stereo is set so that a 2 kHz sound has an intensity of 50 dB when the 2 kHz slider on the equalizer shown is set at 0 dB. Write an inequality that expresses the intensity range that is possible for the sound by moving the 2 kHz slider.

2. An *octave* is the span covered by a 1:2 ratio of frequencies. For example, the span from 1 kHz to 2 kHz is one octave.

    a. Humans can hear sounds ranging from 20 Hz to 20 kHz. If f represents the frequency of sound heard by humans, then the lowest octave heard by humans is 20 Hz $\leq f \leq$ 40 Hz, and the next lowest is 40 Hz $\leq f \leq$ 80 Hz. Continue writing inequalities for successive octaves until you reach approximately 20 kHz. How many octaves does human hearing span?

    b. How are the frequency labels on the equalizer shown related to the inequalities from part (a)?

    c. From part (b), you should have seen that the ten-band equalizer shown spans the 10 octaves of human hearing, and that each slider controls one octave. Would a five-band equalizer give you more or less control than a ten-band equalizer? Why?

6

Equalizers and Inequalities *(Continued)*

Frequency Ranges of Musical Instruments

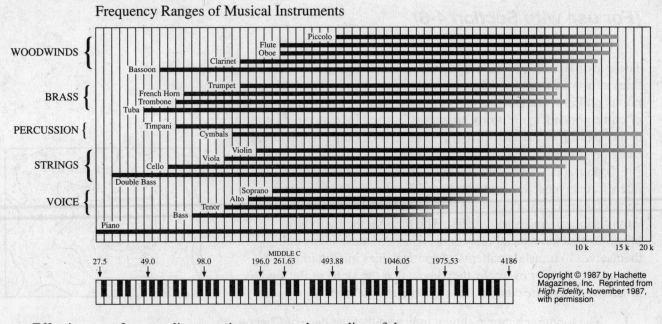

Copyright © 1987 by Hachette Magazines, Inc. Reprinted from *High Fidelity*, November 1987, with permission

Effective use of an equalizer requires some understanding of the frequency ranges of musical instruments. These ranges are shown for various instruments (including the human voice) in the graph above. For example, the piano keyboard below the graph indicates that a piano can play notes with frequencies ranging from 27.5 Hz to 4186 Hz. The graph itself illustrates this range with a dark band (labeled "Piano").

3.   Almost every musical sound consists of a combination of the actual note sounded, called the *fundamental tone*, and a number of tones with higher frequencies, called *overtones*. That is why a piano, for example, can produce sounds with frequencies higher than its highest note. How is this shown in the graph above? What is the approximate range of a piano when overtones are considered?

4.   Write an inequality that approximates the frequency range (including overtones) of each instrument. Also decide which sliders on a ten-band equalizer affect the sounds produced by this instrument.

   a. oboe   **b.** cello   **c.** bass voice   **d.** cymbals

5.   For each of the following bands on a ten-band equalizer, determine which musical instruments are most affected by "boosting" or "cutting" the intensity of the frequencies in the given band.

   a. 8 kHz   **b.** 64 Hz   **c.** 2 kHz   **d.** 250 Hz

6.   Explain why each of the following tips for using a ten-band equalizer makes sense.

   a. To add more punch to a disco beat, "boost" at 32 Hz and 64 Hz.

   b. If voices sound nasal, "cut" at 2 kHz and 4 kHz.

ADVANCED MATHEMATICS
Activities Book

Contour Maps
(For use with Section 4-6)

There are maps of many kinds to help us understand our world. You can think of a typical map, such as a road map, as a correspondence between points on Earth and points on a piece of paper. In fact, because of this kind of correspondence, the word "mapping" is used by mathematicians to refer to any pairing of the elements of two sets. (For example, the squaring function "maps" 2 to 4, −3 to 9, and so on.)

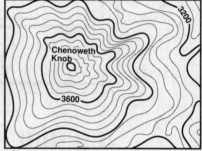

    Topographic maps, like the one shown at the right, are of interest to anyone who needs to know the shape of the terrain in a particular area. Such maps are used by hikers, loggers, transportation planners, and many others. The lines on the map show locations that have equal elevations. Users of these maps train themselves to translate patterns of contour lines into an image of the land itself. For example, they know that the slope of the land is steeper where the contour lines are closer together.

1. The topographic map shown indicates that the base of Chenoweth Knob is about 3400 ft (above sea level). Estimate the maximum elevation of Chenoweth Knob.

    When reading a topographic map, it is helpful to think of elevation as a function of two variables: latitude and longitude. For example, the latitude and longitude of Durham, North Carolina, are about 36°N and 79°W, respectively. Since the elevation of Durham is about 400 ft (above sea level), we have an elevation function e for which e(36°N, 79°W) = 400.

2. Consult an almanac to find the latitude, longitude, and elevation of the city where you live or a city near you.

    When we think of elevation as a function of two variables, we see that the lines on a contour map are just curves of constant elevation. In other words, a contour map shows the cross sections of Earth's surface at various elevations. The following activity will give you the experience of converting a three-dimensional surface into a two-dimensional contour map.

Activity: Making a Contour Map

For this activity you will need an 18 in. × 18 in. piece of plywood, an 18 in. × 18 in. piece of white construction paper, thin cardboard, a sharp knife, finishing nails, a hammer, and a pencil.

    Begin by tacking the construction paper to the plywood. On this plywood-and-paper base, you will build a hilly terrain from layers of cardboard. Using the knife to cut out each layer, make the first layer the largest and each subsequent layer slightly smaller. Alter the outline slightly with each layer so that a "lifelike" hill takes shape as you build up the layers. (For a greater challenge, you may want to build two different hills, with a valley between them.)

ADVANCED MATHEMATICS
Activities Book

Contour Maps *(Continued)*

Experiment until you have the three-dimensional shape that you want. Once you have it, you must use the finishing nails to fix it in place. Making sure that each nail passes through every layer of cardboard, carefully hammer the nails vertically through the cardboard and into the plywood-and-paper base. Since you will be sliding the cardboard off and back onto the nails, be sure that each nail is secure in the plywood and that the head of the nail is a little above the uppermost layer of cardboard.

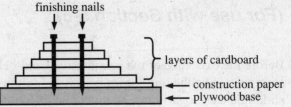

Now make your contour map. Remove all the layers of cardboard except the bottom one. With the pencil, trace the bottom layer's outline on the paper tacked to the plywood. Then remove the bottom layer and put the next-to-the-bottom layer onto the nails so that you can trace its outline. Continue tracing a layer, removing it, and putting on the next one (that is, the layer that is next higher in elevation).

Once the tracing is complete, remove the paper from the plywood and rebuild your original hilly terrain. The paper tracing is a contour map of the terrain.

3. On your contour map, suppose that moving from one contour line to the next up the hill represents a vertical rise of 100 ft.

   a. How far above its base does the hill rise?

   b. If the base of the hill is 1600 ft above sea level, what is the hilltop's elevation (above sea level)?

4. Suppose your hill actually existed and you decided to walk up it. If you wanted to keep your walk as easy as possible, you would follow a path that is less steep than other paths up the hill. Identify such a path on your contour map. What characteristics of the map make it clear that this is the path to take?

5. Suppose you build the same hill but use a different thickness of cardboard. How would your contour map change?

Extensions

Obtain a topographic map of the area where you live and study it to identify familiar landmarks. Use the map to plan a hike.

If you have artistic talent, try drawing a contour map of a human face (with the tip of the nose at the "highest elevation").

9

Logarithms and the Slide Rule
(For use with Section 5-6)

Before the existence of the inexpensive hand-held calculator, students used slide rules, like the one shown below, to multiply and divide numbers. A slide rule uses logarithms, an invention of John Napier (1550–1617) and Henry Briggs (1561–1639), to turn difficult multiplications and divisions into simple additions and subtractions.

After the invention of logarithms came the invention of the logarithmic scale by Edmund Gunter (1581–1626). Gunter was able to perform calculations by using dividers (a device resembling a compass) to add and subtract distances along the logarithmic scale. A few years later, William Oughtred (1574–1660) put two logarithmic scales together (so that one could slide along the other) to create the first linear slide rule.

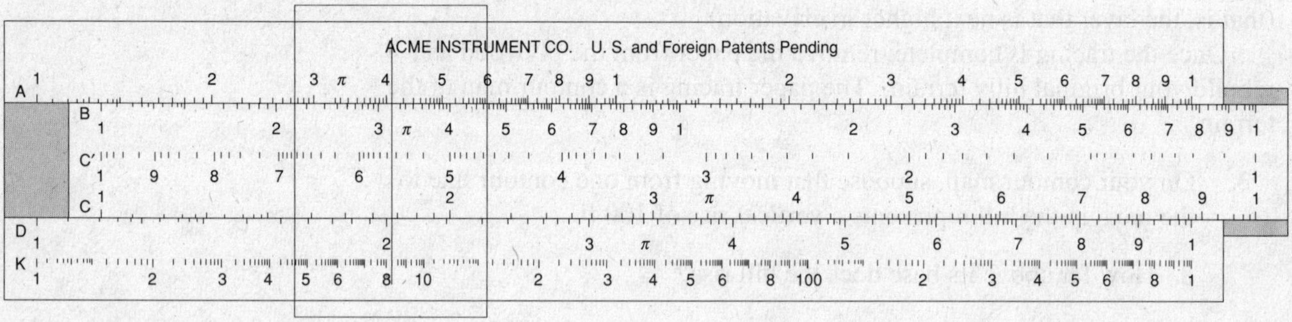

ACME INSTRUMENT CO.   U. S. and Foreign Patents Pending

Logarithmic Scales

Look at the scale shown below. Notice that consecutive integers (1, 2, 3, …) are not evenly spaced. However, the numbers 1, 10, and 100 are. This is due to fact that the scale shown is a base-10 logarithmic scale.

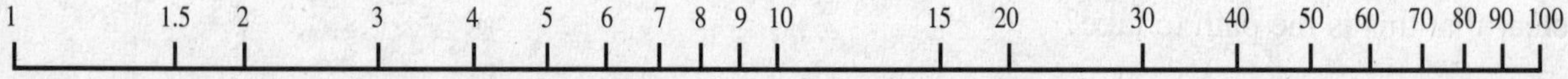

1.   Copy and complete the table below.

Number	1	10	100
Number written as a power of 10	?	?	?
Exponent of number written as a power of 10	?	?	?

As Exercise 1 shows, although 1, 10, and 100 are not consecutive integers, their exponents (when the numbers are written as powers of 10) are. Thus, a unit distance on a base-10 logarithmic scale is not the distance between consecutive integers, but the distance between consecutive integral powers of 10.

ADVANCED MATHEMATICS
Activities Book

Logarithms and the Slide Rule *(Continued)*

2. For a base-10 logarithmic scale, state the mathematical relationship between any number N that appears on the scale and the distance d from the tick mark at 1 to the tick mark at N.

Activity: Making Your Own Slide Rule

For this activity you will need two 5 in. × 8 in. notecards, a centimeter ruler, a pencil, and a calculator.

3. Copy the tables below and use a calculator to complete them. Give each logarithm to the nearest hundredth.

N	$\log N$
1	?
1.5	?
2	?
3	?
4	?

N	$\log N$
5	?
6	?
7	?
8	?
9	?

N	$\log N$
10	?
20	?
30	?
40	?
50	?

N	$\log N$
60	?
70	?
80	?
90	?
100	?

Using the scale 1 cm = 0.1 unit, place tick marks along one of the longer edges of a notecard so that the distances of the tick marks from the left end correspond to the values of $\log N$ from the tables in Exercise 3. Label these tick marks with the corresponding values of N. With the other notecard next to and flush with the first, transfer the tick marks and labels to the other notecard.

One of the laws of logarithms (see page 197 of the text) states that if M and N are positive real numbers, then:

$$\log M + \log N = \log MN$$

This is demonstrated at the right for the specific case of multiplying 2 and 3.

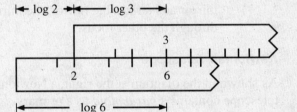

4. Use your slide rule to perform each of the following calculations.

   a. $5 \cdot 10$ **b.** $1.5 \cdot 6$ **c.** $80 \div 2$ **d.** $90 \div 30$

5. Oughtred created a circular slide rule as well as a linear slide rule. The circular slide rule had a pair of moveable pointers attached to a circular card marked with a logarithmic scale. Shown at the right is Oughtred's circular slide rule being used to multiply 2 and 3. Describe what's happening. Then explain how to use the slide rule to divide 6 by 3.

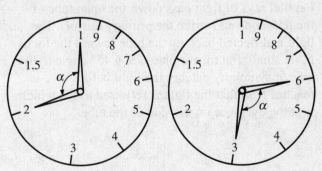

ADVANCED MATHEMATICS
Activities Book

Conics and Telescopes
(For use with Section 6-5)

The stars and planets that are visible from Earth have always fascinated people. Being so far away, however, these celestial bodies were difficult to study until the invention of the telescope about 400 years ago. Through the use of lenses and mirrors, optical telescopes greatly enhance our ability to see into outer space. As the following discussion will show, conics play an important role in the design of telescopes.

1. Suppose a mirrored surface has a cross section in the shape of one branch of a hyperbola. If a ray of light is headed toward the hyperbola's focus behind the mirror, the mirror will reflect the light through the other focus, as shown at the right. Draw a similar diagram for each of the following situations.

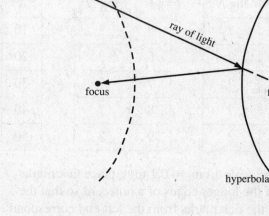

   a. A mirrored surface has a cross section in the shape of a parabola. If a ray of light parallel to the parabola's axis of symmetry strikes the mirror, the mirror will reflect the light through the parabola's focus.

   b. A mirrrored surface has a cross section in the shape of one end of an ellipse. If a ray of light passes through the focus closest to the mirror and strikes the mirror, the mirror will reflect the light through the other focus.

Newtonian Telescope

As shown in the diagram at the right, a Newtonian telescope contains a *paraboloid* as a primary mirror. (A paraboloid is a three-dimensional surface formed by rotating a parabola about its axis of symmetry. Cross sections containing the axis of symmetry are, of course, parabolas.) Parallel rays of light pass down the open tube of the telescope and strike the primary mirror. The light is reflected back up the tube toward the focus F. A small, flat mirror placed at a 45° angle to the axis of symmetry catches the light before it reaches F so that the light is reflected to F', which is at the eyepiece on the side of the tube.

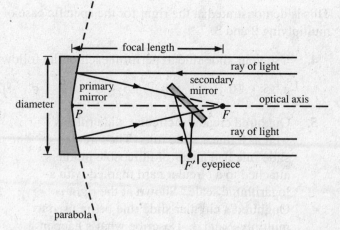

ADVANCED MATHEMATICS
Activities Book

Conics and Telescopes (Continued)

2. The *focal length* of a telescope is the distance between the mirror and the point where the light rays are focused by the mirror. The *focal ratio* is found by dividing the focal length by the diameter of the mirror. For example, if a telescope has a focal length of 48 in. and a mirror diameter of 6 in., then the focal ratio is written f/8.

    a. Find the focal ratio of a telescope with a focal length of 154 in. and a mirror diameter of 14 in.

    b. The 200 in. Hale telescope on Mt. Palomar in California is so large that the observer sits in a basket at the focal point inside the telescope. The focal ratio of the Hale telescope is f/3.3. How far from the mirror does the observer sit? Give your answer in inches and then in feet.

Gregorian Telescope

As shown in the diagram at the right, a Gregorian telescope contains a paraboloid as the primary mirror and an *ellipsoid* (see Exercise 29 on page 230 of the text) as a secondary mirror. Parallel rays of light strike the primary mirror and are reflected through the primary focus, F_1, to the secondary mirror. Since F_1 is a focus of the ellipsoid as well as the paraboloid, the light is then reflected to the second focus of the ellipsoid, F_2, which is at the eyepiece.

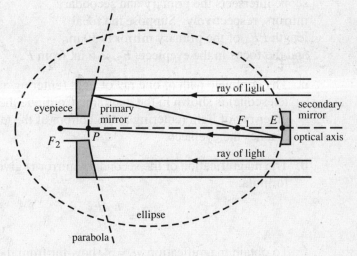

3. In the diagram, note that P and E are the points where the optical axis of the telescope intersects the primary and secondary mirrors, respectively. Suppose the focal length PF_1 of the primary mirror is 30 in., and the focus in the eyepiece, F_2, is 6 in. from P.

    a. The complete path of one ray of light (entering at the top of the telescope) is shown in the diagram. Continue the path of the other ray of light (entering at the bottom of the telescope) until it reaches the eyepiece.

    b. The magnification of the secondary mirror is given by the formula:

    $$m = \frac{F_2E}{F_1E}$$

    To obtain magnification $m = 5$, how far from the primary focus F_1 should the secondary mirror be placed?

ADVANCED MATHEMATICS
Activities Book

Conics and Telescopes (Continued)

Cassegrain Telescope

As shown in the diagram at the right, a Cassegrain telescope contains a paraboloid as the primary mirror and a *hyperboloid* (see Exercise 25 on page 236 of the text) as a secondary mirror. Parallel rays of light strike the primary mirror and are reflected toward the primary focus, F_1, and intercepted by the secondary mirror. Since F_1 is a focus of the hyperboloid as well as the paraboloid, the light is then reflected to the second focus of the hyperboloid, F_2, which is at the eyepiece.

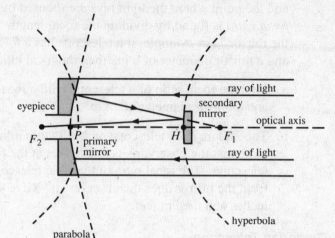

4. In the diagram, note that P and H are the points where the optical axis of the telescope intersects the primary and secondary mirrors, respectively. Suppose the focal length PF_1 of the primary mirror is 30 in., and the focus in the eyepiece, F_2, is 6 in. from P.

   a. The complete path of one ray of light (entering at the top of the telescope) is shown in the diagram. Continue the path of the other ray of light (entering at the bottom of the telescope) until it reaches the eyepiece.

   b. The magnification of the secondary mirror is given by the formula:

   $$m = \frac{F_2H}{F_1H}$$

   To obtain magnification $m = 4$, how far from the primary focus F_1 should the secondary mirror be placed?

5. The diagram at the right is a cross-sectional composite of the three types of reflecting telescopes that we have discussed. A coordinate system has been placed on the diagram so that the x-axis coincides with the telescopes' common optical axis and the origin is halfway between F_1 and F_2. If $F_1F_2 = 36$ in., $F_2P = 6$ in., $F_1E = 9$ in., and $F_1H = 7.2$ in., use the scale 1 unit = 1 inch (on both axes) to find an equation of (a) the parabola, (b) the ellipse, and (c) the hyperbola.

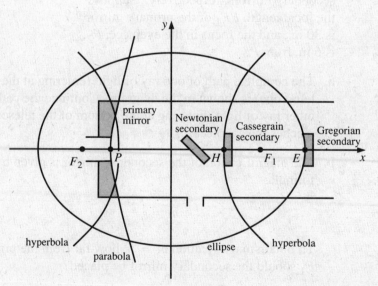

Equation Solving in Ancient Civilizations
(For use with Section 6-6)

While the general theory of polynomial equations was developed relatively
recently (see page 88 of the text), mathematicians have been interested in
solving cubic and higher-degree equations for thousands of years.

Cubic Equations in Babylonia

Although nothing akin to algebraic notation existed in ancient Babylonia
(about 1800 B.C.), the oldest indications of an interest in cubic equations
are found there in the tables of values that were calculated for expressions
such as $n^3 + n^2$. The beginning of such a table is shown at the right. A
solution of an equation like $n^3 + n^2 = 22$ could be estimated from the
table, and then improved upon by trial and error. In the example below,
we look at a more complicated equation that can be solved using this table.

n	$n^3 + n^2$
1	2
1.5	5.625
2	12
2.5	21.875
3	36

Example   Solve for x: $9x^3 + 3x^2 = 4$

Solution   In order to use the table for $n^3 + n^2$, the equation must be put in the form
$n^3 + n^2 = c$, where c is a constant. We make the first term a perfect cube
by multiplying both sides of the equation by 3:

$$27x^3 + 9x^2 = 12$$

Note that multiplying by 3 also makes the second term a perfect square.
Letting $n = 3x$, we can rewrite the equation as $n^3 + n^2 = 12$. The solution of this equation, $n = 2$, is read from the table above. Since $n = 3x$,
we have $x = \frac{2}{3}$ as a solution of the original equation.

---

1. Show that the equation in the example has no other real solutions.

2. Discuss the limitations of this method of solving a cubic equation.

3. Use the method of the example to solve $2x^3 + x^2 = 20$.

Cubic Equations in Greece and Persia

The use of algebraic symbols and methods in Greece did not begin until the
3rd century A.D. In the 3rd and 4th centuries B.C., however, Archimedes
and Menæchmus solved some cubic equations by purely geometric means
that involved finding intersection points of conic sections. During the 9th
through 12th centuries A.D., Arab mathematicians, using a system more
clearly recognizable as algebra, made considerable advances with the Greek
methods. The most significant Arab work was done by a Persian, Omar
Khayyam (about 1100), who presented methods of solving, for positive
roots only, thirteen categories of cubic equations. We now consider an
equation from one of these categories.

---

15   ADVANCED MATHEMATICS
                                                              Activities Book

Equation Solving in Ancient Civilizations *(Continued)*

Khayyam solved cubic equations of the form $x^3 + b^2x = b^2c$ by finding the intersection point(s) of the parabola $x^2 = by$ and the circle $y^2 = x(c - x)$. For example, if $b = 2$ and $c = 3$, the cubic equation is $x^3 + 4x = 12$, the parabola is $x^2 = 2y$, and the circle is $y^2 = x(3 - x)$. The following exercises will help you understand how the method worked.

4. **a.** To transform the cubic equation into the equations of the parabola and the circle, begin by multiplying both sides of the equation $x^3 + 4x = 12$ by x, $x \neq 0$. Show that your new equation can be rewritten in the form $\frac{x^2}{2} = \pm\sqrt{x(3 - x)}$.

    b. What steps would you use to separate the last equation of part (a) into the two equations $x^2 = 2y$ and $y^2 = x(3 - x)$?

5. Show that $y^2 = x(3 - x)$ is the equation of a circle by rewriting it in center-radius form. (You will need to complete the square.)

6. **a.** On the same set of axes, graph the parabola $x^2 = 2y$ and the circle $y^2 = x(3 - x)$. Use your graph to estimate the solution of the cubic equation $x^3 + 4x = 12$.

    b. The intersection point $(0, 0)$ does not correspond to a root of the equation $x^3 + 4x = 12$. At what point in the solution was the extraneous root $x = 0$ introduced?

Higher-Degree Equations in China

By the time of Khayyam's classification of cubic equations, Chinese mathematicians were working on methods of approximating roots of higher-degree equations. In the mid-11th century, Jiǎ Xiàn developed a procedure for calculating nth roots of numbers, a procedure not discovered in Europe for another 800 years. In the 12th century, Líu Yì succeeded in applying Jiǎ Xiàn's method to the solution of higher-degree equations.

7. Pictured at the right is the earliest known example of an equation solved by Líu Yì's method. The equation is written as it would have been in 12th century China. Here is the equation in modern notation:

    $$-5x^4 + 52x^3 + 128x^2 - 4096 = 0$$

    As was true in all civilizations that did early work on higher-degree equations, the Chinese sought only one solution. Try to find a small positive integer that is a solution of the above equation.

8. Find one or more solutions of each of these equations from the Chinese text *Mathematical Treatise in Nine Sections* (1247).

    a. $-x^4 + 763{,}200x^2 - 40{,}642{,}560{,}000 = 0$

    b. $x^{10} + 15x^8 + 72x^6 - 864x^4 - 11{,}664x^2 - 34{,}992 = 0$

ADVANCED MATHEMATICS
Activities Book

Working with Radians
(For use with Section 7-2)

Why Radian Measure?

As you begin your study of trigonometry, you may be annoyed at having to learn about radians, an entirely new way of measuring angles. Degree measure, learned and used over several years, is probably difficult to let go. You may be tempted to keep thinking in degree measure despite the advantages of thinking in radian measure. We all have a good idea of what a 60° angle looks like, what a 90° angle looks like, and so on, and it may seem pointless to adopt a new system. So why make the change?

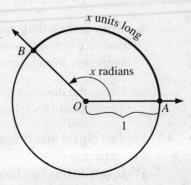

There are good reasons for using radian measure. While the degree measure of an angle tells us the fraction of a complete revolution that the angle represents (for example, a 90° angle represents $\frac{90}{360} = \frac{1}{4}$ of a revolution), the radian measure of an angle tells us the length of the arc intercepted by the angle when it is a central angle of a unit circle. In other words, radian measure ties angular measurement to linear measurement. In the diagram of the unit circle with center O and central angle AOB, x represents both the measure of angle AOB and the length of arc AB.

1. In the diagram, if the measure of angle AOB is x degrees instead of x radians, what is the length of arc AB?

The direct correspondence between angular and linear measurement when radian measure is used simplifies many mathematical and physical formulas (see, for example, the discussion on page 263 of the text). It also breaks the link between angles and trigonometric functions. That is, when evaluating a trigonometric function of x (in radians), we do not need to think of x as the measure of an angle; we can simply treat x as a real number. This is particularly useful in working with trigonometric models of periodic phenomena (to be discussed in Chapter 8). For example, a function like $d(t) = -\cos t$ might be used to describe the displacement d at time t (note that t is not an angular measure!) of a weight attached to an anchored coil spring as the weight oscillates after being pulled down and then released.

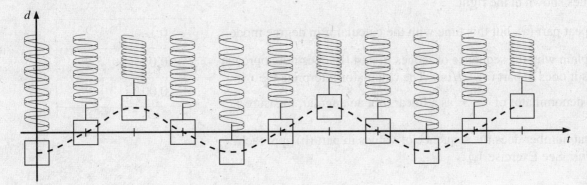

ADVANCED MATHEMATICS
Activities Book

Working with Radians (Continued)

Activity 1: Radian Measure and Apparent Size

This activity will help you become accustomed to radian measure. You will need a measuring tape, scissors, and some stiff cardboard.

First, holding your right arm perpendicular to your body and pointing your fingers up, have someone measure the distance from your right eye to a fingertip. Then cut out a strip of cardboard with a length equal to your eye-to-fingertip distance. Now, with your arm again outstretched, hold the strip so that it is parallel to your body and its center is at eye level.

2. The angle that your eye makes with the ends of the strip is about 1 radian. Explain why.

3. a. Draw a scale diagram showing your eye, the strip, and the distance between your eye and the strip. Also draw line segments from your eye to the ends of the strip.

   b. Using the diagram from part (a), determine whether your approximation of 1 radian is too large or too small.

4. Find an object that is farther than arm's length from you and that has the same apparent size (see page 264 of the text) as the radian strip. (You can do this by choosing a nearby object and then moving either closer to or farther from the object until its top and bottom match the ends of the strip.) Now, measure the distance from you to the object, and use the formula for apparent size to approximate the object's actual size.

5. Exercise 4 can be done without any reference to radian measure. Draw a diagram showing your eye, the strip in your hand, and the object being measured. By referring to the diagram, explain how plane geometry can be used to find the object's size.

Activity 2: Degree and Radian Measure on a Calculator

In Chapter 19, you will learn that the value of the ratio $\frac{\sin x}{x}$ approaches 1 as the value of x approaches 0 (see Exercise 43 on page 725 of the text).

6. a. Using a calculator set in radian mode, complete the table of values shown at the right.

   b. Repeat part (a), but this time with the calculator in degree mode.

   c. Explain why the sequence of values in part (b) does not approach 1 as it does in part (a). (*Hint*: The calculator interprets the x in the denominator of $\frac{\sin x}{x}$ as a linear, not an angular, measure.)

   d. What number does the sequence of values in part (b) approach? (*Hint*: See Exercise 1.)

x	$\frac{\sin x}{x}$
0.1	?
0.01	?
0.001	?

Making Waves
(For use with Section 8-2)

As you have seen in your text, sine waves are often encountered when periodic or oscillatory phenomena—such as temperatures, tides, and electricity—are studied. The following activities will give you two different ways to create sine waves artificially.

Activity 1: Paper Slicing

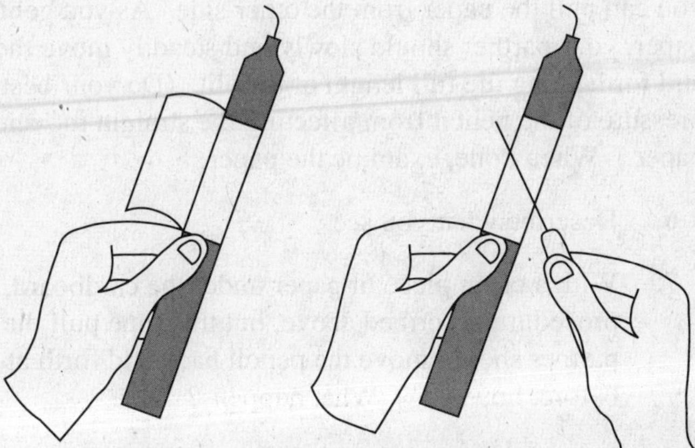

For this activity you will need three sheets of paper, three candles (two with the same diameter and one with a smaller diameter), some tape, a cutting board, and a sharp knife.

As shown at the right, tightly roll a sheet of paper around one of the two candles having the same diameter, and then tape the paper so that it will not unwind. Place the candle on the cutting board, and position the knife on top of the candle so that the knife's blade makes a 45° angle with the candle's wick line and points *away* from the hand holding the candle. Then, pushing the blade *toward the cutting board*, slice (or gently saw) through the paper and candle. When you are done, remove the tape and unwind the paper.

1. Describe what you see.

2. Using the candle having the smaller diameter, repeat the procedure described above. Again, describe what you see. How does changing the diameter affect the result of this activity?

3. Using the last of the three candles, repeat the procedure described above, but this time hold the knife so that the blade makes a 30° angle with the wick line of the candle. Again, describe what you see. How does changing the angle affect the result of this activity?

4. Relate all that you have done to the concepts of frequency (the number of cycles per sheet of paper) and amplitude. Describe what you must do to increase or decrease frequency and amplitude.

5. *Extension* Without using a candle, roll up a piece of paper and then flatten it. Use scissors to make a straight cut obliquely across the paper. After unfolding the paper, describe what you see. How must you cut the paper in order to make the result look like a sine wave?

ADVANCED MATHEMATICS
Activities Book

Making Waves (Continued)

Activity 2: Paper Sliding

For this activity you should work with a partner. You and your partner will need several sheets of paper, some tape, a pencil, scissors (or a knife), and a piece of cardboard about 10 cm × 40 cm.

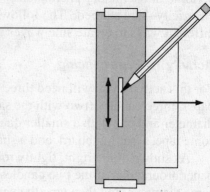

As indicated in the diagram at the right, make a narrow slit in the cardboard; a pencil needs to move back and forth across the slit without wobbling. Tape the ends of the cardboard to a flat surface, and slide a piece of paper under the cardboard just far enough so that you can pull the paper from the other side. As you gently pull the paper, your partner should slowly and steadily move the pencil back and forth along the full length of the slit. (Do your best to keep the pressure of the pencil from affecting the straight movement of the paper.) When done, examine the paper.

6. Describe what you see.

7. With a clean piece of paper under the cardboard, repeat the procedure described above, but this time pull the paper faster. (Your partner should move the pencil back and forth at the same rate as before, however.) What happens?

8. In light of Exercise 7, describe (and then try) another way to increase the frequency (the number of cycles per sheet of paper) of the sine wave that results from this activity.

9. How would you change the amplitude of the sine wave that results from this activity?

ADVANCED MATHEMATICS
Activities Book

NAME _____   DATE _____

Circles and Spheres in Architecture
(For use with Section 9-2)

In many countries and cultures, circular and spherical forms have long
played an important role in architecture. Examples are many and varied:
the cylindrical shape of medieval castle towers in western Europe and of
some West African houses; the cone shape of Native American tepees;
the dome shape of igloos, geodesic domes, and Middle Eastern mosques;
the circular or oval shape of Pueblo Indian kivas (ceremonial chambers),
of central Asian yurts, and of sports stadiums, both ancient and modern.

1. What factors might influence decisions about architectural form in
    various regions of the world? What architectural advantages do you
    think circular shapes have?

   The best architects and engineers try to use a minimum of resources to
achieve their design goals, such as enclosing the largest amount of space,
creating the most energy-efficient structure, or giving a building its greatest
structural strength. The following exercise, which considers the problem of
how to maximize enclosed space, will help you understand one reason
architects and builders in so many cultures use circular shapes.

2. The dome-shaped structure shown at the right is a hemisphere of
    radius 10 m, and the rectangular structure is a cube.

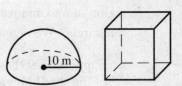

   a. If the dome and cube have equal surface areas, find the volume
       of each. (Do not include the "floor" as part of either structure's
       surface area.) Which structure has more space inside? Is there
       another shape of equal surface area having greater volume?

   b. If the dome and the cube have floors with equal perimeters, find
       the area of each floor. Which structure has more floor space?

   The results of Exercise 2 may lead you to conjecture that for a given
surface area, a sphere encloses the maximum volume, and for a given
perimeter, a circle encloses the maximum area. These conjectures are true,
and are known as the *isoperimetric property* of the sphere and of the circle.
Let's prove the two-dimensional case of this property.

Theorem   For a given perimeter, the curve enclosing the maximum area is a circle.

   The proof of the isoperimetric property has three important parts:
1. We show that the curve with maximum area must be *convex*, that is,
   any segment joining two points of the curve lies entirely inside or on
   the curve.
2. We show that a segment dividing the curve into two pieces equal in
   length separates the interior of the curve into two regions equal in area.
3. We show that each of the regions is semicircular.

21

ADVANCED MATHEMATICS
Activities Book

Circles and Spheres in Architecture *(Continued)*

Each part of the proof uses indirect reasoning, also called *proof by contradiction*, in which we assume that what we want to prove is false, and then show how this assumption leads to a contradiction.

3. Let *C* be the curve of fixed perimeter *P* enclosing maximum area. To prove that *C* must be convex, first suppose *C* is *not* convex, as shown in the diagram. Draw $\overline{AB}$ lying entirely outside *C* and consider the reflection in $\overline{AB}$ of the portion of *C* between *A* and *B*. What contradiction arises in considering the new curve *C′*?

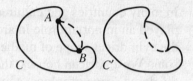

4. As shown at the right, pick a point *X* on *C* and go halfway around *C* to point *Y* so that these points divide *C* into two curves of equal length. Since *C* must be convex, $\overline{XY}$ divides the interior of *C* into two regions. Explain why these two regions must have equal areas. (*Hint*: Suppose the regions have *unequal* areas. Reflect the region of greater area in $\overline{XY}$, and compare the area enclosed by this new curve to the area enclosed by *C*. What contradiction arises?)

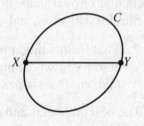

5. Exercise 4 permits us to shift our focus from showing that *C* is a circle to showing that half of *C* is a semicircle. Thus, if *O* is an arbitrary point on *C* and if $\overarc{XOY}$ (with length $\frac{1}{2}P$) and $\overline{XY}$ enclose a region of maximum area, then we need to show that $\overarc{XOY}$ is a semicircle. We begin by showing that $\angle XOY$ is a right angle.

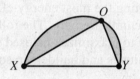

   a. Suppose $\angle XOY$ is *not* a right angle. Without changing the areas of the shaded regions or the length of $\overarc{XOY}$ in the figure above, draw a new figure with $\angle X'OY' = 90°$, as shown at the right. (To do so, imagine that the shaded regions are hinged at point *O*; then adjust their positions until $\angle X'OY'$ is a right angle.) Show that area($\triangle X'OY'$) > area($\triangle XOY$). What contradiction arises?

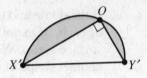

   b. Knowing that $\angle XOY$ is a right angle, show that $\overarc{XOY}$ is a semicircle and, therefore, that *C* is a circle. (*Hint*: As shown in the diagram, consider the midpoint *M* of $\overline{XY}$ and the distance *OM*.)

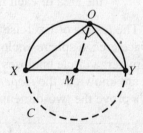

The following exercises suggest applications of the isoperimetric property of circles and spheres to architectural decisions.

6. Use the isoperimetric property of circles and spheres to explain why so many storage facilities, such as grain silos and water towers, are either cylindrical or spherical in shape.

7. a. Suppose that instead of maximizing volume using a given surface area, you want to minimize surface area using a given volume. What shape would you choose? Why?

   b. Heat loss from a building is proportional to the surface area of the building. Explain why a dome shape is a practical choice for the shape of an igloo.

ADVANCED MATHEMATICS
Activities Book

Mathematicians of Alexandria
(For use with Section 9-4)

In the fourth century B.C., the city of Alexandria, located near the mouth of the Nile River in Africa, became the political, economic, and intellectual center of the ancient world. Alexandria's second ruler, Ptolemy, founded the city's famous library and established a school where intellectuals from many different countries met to share ideas. The city thus developed an unusually diverse population; people of Egyptian, Ethiopian, and other African backgrounds as well as people of Greek, Jewish, Roman, and Arab backgrounds all intermingled in Alexandrian society.

Because of their city's importance as a trade center, Alexandrian mathematicians were constantly searching for more efficient and accurate solutions to problems of navigation. They also worked on other practical problems, such as map-making, calendar refinement, military technology, mechanics, the use of materials, and production efficiency.

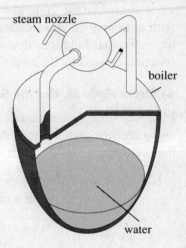

Hero, a notable Alexandrian mathematician and inventor, was of Egyptian heritage and lived in the first century A.D. He wrote prolifically on such subjects as civil engineering, mechanics, optics, and measurement. He described, for example, how to dig tunnels under mountains by working from both ends at the same time. He also wrote a commentary on Euclid's *Elements* and proved new theorems for finding areas (see Exercise 26 on page 354 of the text). His ingenious mechanical inventions included a simple steam engine (pictured at the right) and a tiny windmill, both of which are the earliest known examples of these technologies.

Another prominent Alexandrian was Hypatia (about 370–415 A.D.), who was a popular lecturer on mathematics, philosophy, astronomy, and mechanics. She wrote commentaries on the work of other mathematicians (such as Diophantus and Apollonius) and used these commentaries as text-books for her students. She also invented a number of scientific instruments, including an astrolabe (for measuring the positions of stars and planets) and a hydroscope (for viewing underwater objects).

Research Project

Research and give a presentation to the class on the life and accomplishments of other great mathematicians of Alexandria. Among those whose achievements warrant further investigation are: Archimedes, Eratosthenes, Nicomedes, Menelaus, Diophantus, and Pappus.

For further information, you may wish to consult the following:

Kline, Morris. *Mathematical Thought from Ancient to Modern Times.* New York: Oxford University Press, 1972.

Hogben, Lancelot. *Mathematics in the Making.* Garden City, New York: Doubleday, 1960.

Newman, James, ed. *The World of Mathematics, Volume I.* New York: Simon and Schuster, 1956.

Struik, Dirk. *A Concise History of Mathematics.* New York: Dover, 1967.

23

Sums of Sine Waves
(For use with Section 10-1)

As you saw in Chapter 8, tidal motion is an example of a periodic phenomenon to which trigonometric functions can be applied. Not all tides behave as simply as the tides described in Example 2 on page 311 of the text, however. The graph shown at the right also represents periodic variation in water depth over time, but the curve is not a simple sine wave. In fact, the water depth here is influenced by two tidal motions and can be modeled with an equation involving the sum of two sine (or cosine) functions. In this activity we will explore the graphs of sums of sine and/or cosine functions, with our focus on understanding how the periods and amplitudes of the individual functions determine the period and amplitude of the function created by their sum.

Different Periods, But the Same Amplitude

First we will consider functions of the form $h(x) = f(x) + g(x)$, where f and g are sine and/or cosine functions with the same amplitude. How do the periods of f and g determine the period of h?

1. Copy and complete the table below. Use a computer or graphing calculator to graph h in order to determine the period of h.

	Functions		Period of f	Period of g	Period of $h(x) = f(x) + g(x)$
	$f(x) = \sin \pi x$	$g(x) = \cos \frac{\pi}{2}x$	2	4	4
a.	$f(x) = 2 \sin \pi x$	$g(x) = -2 \cos \frac{2\pi}{3}x$	?	?	?
b.	$f(x) = -\cos 2\pi x$	$g(x) = \cos \frac{3\pi}{2}x$	?	?	?
c.	$f(x) = 3 \sin 2x$	$g(x) = 3 \sin 3x$	?	?	?

2. On the basis of your results in Exercise 1, draw a general conclusion about the relationship between the period of $h(x) = f(x) + g(x)$ and the periods of f and g. Explain your reasoning and give some other specific examples to support your conclusion.

Different Amplitudes, But the Same Period

Now we consider the graphs of functions of the form $h(x) = f(x) + g(x)$, where f and g are sine and/or cosine functions with the same period. How do the amplitudes of f and g determine the amplitude of h?

ADVANCED MATHEMATICS
Activities Book

Sums of Sine Waves *(Continued)*

3. Copy and complete the table below. Use a computer or graphing calculator to graph h in order to determine the amplitude of h.

	Functions		Amplitude of f	Amplitude of g	Amplitude of $h(x) = f(x) + g(x)$
	$f(x) = 3 \sin x$	$g(x) = 4 \cos x$	3	4	5
a.	$f(x) = 12 \cos x$	$g(x) = -5 \sin x$	?	?	?
b.	$f(x) = -0.7 \cos x$	$g(x) = -2.4 \sin x$	?	?	?
c.	$f(x) = 8 \sin 2x$	$g(x) = -6 \cos 2x$	?	?	?

4. On the basis of your results in Exercise 3, draw a general conclusion about the relationship between the amplitude of $h(x) = f(x) + g(x)$ and the amplitudes of f and g. Confirm your conclusion by looking at other specific examples.

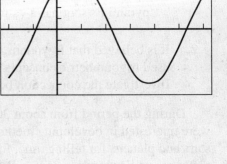

In completing Exercise 3, you should have noticed that the graph of each function h is a simple sine wave. For example, as the simulated graphing calculator screen at the right shows, the graph of the function $h(x) = 3 \sin x + 4 \cos x$ is a sine wave that is horizontally shifted. Since the amplitude of h is 5, the equation of h can be written in the form $h(x) = 5 \sin (x - C)$, where C is the horizontal shift. To find a value for C, we can use the difference formula for sine (see page 370 of the text):

$$h(x) = 5 \sin (x - C)$$
$$= 5(\sin x \cos C - \cos x \sin C)$$
$$= (5 \cos C) \sin x + (-5 \sin C) \cos x$$

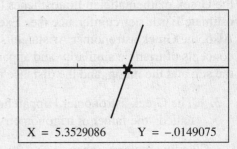

X = 5.3529086   Y = -.0149075

By equating corresponding constants in $h(x) = 3 \sin x + 4 \cos x$ and $h(x) = (5 \cos C) \sin x + (-5 \sin C) \cos x$, we obtain the equations $3 = 5 \cos C$ and $4 = -5 \sin C$, or $0.6 = \cos C$ and $-0.8 = \sin C$. This pair of equations has the solution $C \approx 5.35$ in the interval $0 \le C < 2\pi$; therefore, the equation of h is $h(x) = 5 \sin (x - 5.35)$. Using the zoom and trace features of a graphing calculator (as shown at the right), we can confirm that the horizontal shift is about 5.35 by locating the first point to the right of the origin where the graph of h crosses the x-axis and then rises above the x-axis as x increases.

5. For each function h in Exercise 3, use the procedure described above to find the horizontal shift. Then write the equation of h in the form $h(x) = A \sin B(x - C)$. Confirm your value for the horizontal shift by using the zoom and trace features of a graphing calculator.

6. Let $f(x) = A_1 \sin x$ and $g(x) = A_2 \cos x$. Use the procedure described above to show that the amplitude of $h(x) = f(x) + g(x)$ is $\sqrt{(A_1)^2 + (A_2)^2}$.

ADVANCED MATHEMATICS
Activities Book

History of Trigonometry
(For use with Section 10-3)

Trigonometry, the study of triangle measurements, had its beginnings more than 4000 years ago in ancient Egypt. The most famous of Egyptian writings on mathematics is the Rhind papyrus, written about 1650 B.C.

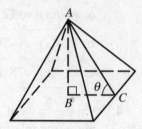

1. Among other things, the Rhind papyrus describes the "seqt" of a pyramid's lateral face. The seqt was given as the ratio of the horizontal run (*BC* in the diagram) to the vertical rise (*AB* in the diagram). The run was expressed in hands, and the rise was expressed in cubits (with 1 cubit = 7 hands).

    a. What is the mathematical relationship between the seqt and the modern concept of slope?

    b. Use the diagram to show that a pyramid's seqt is equal to $\dfrac{\cot \theta}{7}$.

    c. The Rhind papyrus describes a pyramid that is 250 cubits high and has a square base that is 360 cubits on a side. Show that the pyramid's seqt has a value of $5\dfrac{1}{25}$ hands per cubit.

2. It is believed that Egyptians, Babylonians, Greeks, and Arabs all used trigonometric concepts in their construction of sundials. Investigate the connection between sundials and trigonometry.

   During the period from about 300 B.C. to A.D. 200, Greek astronomers were interested in developing methods for predicting the positions of the stars and planets, for telling time, for navigating, and for estimating distances on Earth and in space. Practical concerns like these led to the development of many trigonometric concepts and techniques. For example, the Greek mathematician Eratosthenes (about 276–194 B.C.) was able to estimate Earth's circumference (see Exercise 16 on page 266 of the text). Also, the Greek astronomer Aristarchus (about 310–230 B.C.) used the concepts of triangle similarity and apparent size to estimate the diameters of the sun and the moon, and the distance of each from Earth.

3. The Greek astronomer Hipparchus (about 180–125 B.C.) has been called "the father of trigonometry." Find out why.

   Claudius Ptolemy (about A.D. 100–165), an Egyptian astronomer and geographer, summarized and extended Hipparchus' work in trigonometry in a book that Arab scholars later called *Almagest* ("The Greatest"). By using the theorem now known as "Ptolemy's theorem" (see Exercise 44 on page 374 of the text) while working with arcs of a circle and the chords connecting the endpoints of the arcs, Ptolemy was able to find formulas for sin ($\alpha \pm \beta$) and cos ($\alpha \pm \beta$). He was also able to develop "half-arc" formulas, the equivalent of our half-angle formulas.

ADVANCED MATHEMATICS
Activities Book

History of Trigonometry *(Continued)*

Ptolemy's method of computation was based on the sexagesimal, or base 60, number system. The radius of a circle was divided into 60 parts (that is, 1 radius $= 60^p$), with each part divided into 60 minutes ($1^p = 60'$) and each minute divided into 60 seconds ($1' = 60''$). The circumference of the circle was divided into 360 degrees. Using this system, Ptolemy created a table of chord lengths for arcs from $\frac{1}{2}^\circ$ to 180° in steps of $\frac{1}{2}^\circ$. This table was an essential tool of astronomers for a thousand years after Ptolemy.

4. In Ptolemy's system, the chord length for a 90° arc, written cd 90°, was expressed as $84^p\ 51'\ 10''$. Compare this value with the exact length, $60\sqrt{2}$.

5. Using Ptolemy's system, what is cd 60°?

6. Use the diagram at the right to show that $\sin \alpha = \dfrac{\text{cd } 2\alpha}{120}$.
    Thus, Ptolemy's table was equivalent to a table of sines for
    angles from $\frac{1}{4}^\circ$ to 90° in steps of $\frac{1}{4}^\circ$.

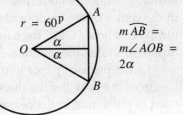

One of trigonometry's primary strengths is that it allows us to make indirect measurements. For example, if you stand at the top of a mountain that is 2 mi high and measure the angle β formed by the line of sight to the horizon and the line from the mountaintop to Earth's center, then you can compute Earth's radius R simply by solving the equation $\sin \beta = \dfrac{R}{R + 2}$. Even after 4000 years, trigonometry continues to be important in many fields, including surveying, astronomy, and mapmaking.

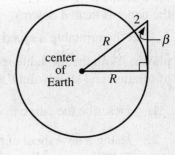

7. Choose one of the following mathematicians and investigate his contribution to the development of trigonometry.

    a. Hindu mathematician Aryabhata (about A.D. 475–550)

    b. French mathematician François Viète (1540–1603)

For further investigation of the history of trigonometry, you may wish to consult the following:

Boyer, Carl B. and Uta C. Merzbach. *A History of Mathematics.*
New York: John Wiley & Sons, 1989.

Eves, Howard. *Great Moments in Mathematics (Before 1650).*
Washington, D.C.: Mathematical Association of America, 1983.

Kennedy, Edward S. "The History of Trigonometry" in *Historical Topics for the Mathematics Classroom.* 2nd ed. Reston, VA: National Council of Teachers of Mathematics, 1989.

Resnikoff, H. L. and R. O. Wells, Jr. *Mathematics in Civilization.*
New York: Dover, 1984.

ADVANCED MATHEMATICS
Activities Book

Spirals
(For use with Section 11-1)

Spirals show up in some interesting and diverse places—in seashells, in
sunflowers, and in the shape of galaxies, for example. The following
activity gives you an opportunity to make spirals of your own.

Activity: Making Spirals

For this activity you will need a record player with a working turntable, a
piece of cardboard to cover the turntable, scissors, unlined paper, tacks,
tape, and a felt-tipped pen.

   Cut out a square of cardboard big enough to cover the record player's
turntable without interfering with the turntable's motion. Put a small hole
in the center of the cardboard so that you can place the cardboard on the
turntable's post. Once the cardboard is in position, carefully tape it to the
turntable so that the cardboard will not slip when the turntable is spinning.

   Tack a piece of paper to the cardboard. (Depending on the
length of the post and the thickness of the cardboard, you may
need to put a hole in the center of the paper before tacking it to
the cardboard. If not, mark on the paper where the post is once
the paper is tacked down.)

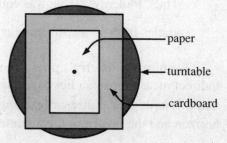

   Set the turntable's speed at $33\frac{1}{3}$ rpm, and turn on the record
player. With the turntable spinning, put the pen down at the center
of rotation and slowly draw the pen toward you in a "straight" line.

1. Describe the curve that you get.

2. Using a new sheet of paper, repeat the procedure described above,
    but this time pull the pen more quickly toward you. How does the
    new curve differ from the first?

3. Determine what happens when you move the pen *very* slowly.

4. Now vary the speed of the turntable. (The turntable should at least
    have a speed of 45 rpm; some older turntables also have speeds of
    16 rpm and 78 rpm. Try them all!) At each turntable speed that you
    try, do your best to move the pen toward you at the same steady rate.
    How do the various speeds affect the resulting curves?

5. Normally, it's very easy to draw a straight line. Imagine, however,
    that you want to draw a straight line on a piece of paper as it spins.
    Describe the pen motion that you would need to use in order to draw
    the line. Try it!

6. Normally, it's difficult to draw a good circle. What do you have to
    do to draw a circle on a piece of paper as it spins? Try it!

ADVANCED MATHEMATICS
Activities Book

Spirals *(Continued)*

7. **a.** Suppose you marked a piece of paper with two points, as shown
    at the right, and wanted to connect the points—with the paper
    spinning—in *one* revolution of the turntable. Predict the curve
    that would result. Then confirm your prediction by carrying out
    the experiment.

    b. Repeat part (a) using other pairs of points. (If the points are not
collinear with the center of rotation, you should be able to
connect them in less than one revolution of the turntable.) Are
there any point pairs that are easier to connect than others?

8. When space probes like *Voyager* are launched to rendezvous with
    other planets, the paths that they travel from Earth to their targets
    often look like the ones you obtained in Exercise 7. Investigate
    such interplanetary flight paths, and draw a diagram of a particular
    probe's path from Earth to its target planet.

ADVANCED MATHEMATICS
Activities Book

Friction
(For use with Section 12-2)

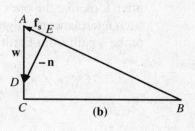
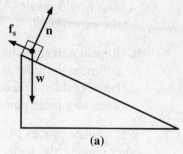

Three forces act on an object when it is at rest on an inclined plane:

$\mathbf{f_s}$ = the static-friction force (the resistance to sliding down the plane)
$\mathbf{w}$ = the weight force (the pull of gravity on the object)
$\mathbf{n}$ = the normal force (the push of the plane on the object)

Figure (a) shows these three forces. Note that $\mathbf{f_s}$ acts parallel to the plane, $\mathbf{w}$ acts straight down, and $\mathbf{n}$ acts perpendicular to the plane.

Since the object is not moving, the three forces acting on it are in *equilibrium*; that is, $\mathbf{f_s} + \mathbf{n} + \mathbf{w} = \mathbf{0}$, or

$$\mathbf{f_s} + \mathbf{w} = -\mathbf{n}.$$

Figure (b) illustrates this last equation.

1. Use figure (b) to show that $\triangle ADE \sim \triangle ABC$.

Exercise 1 allows us to conclude that $\dfrac{AE}{DE} = \dfrac{AC}{BC}$. Note that $AE = |\mathbf{f_s}|$ and $DE = |-\mathbf{n}|$. If we let $AC = y =$ rise of the plane, and $BC = x =$ run of the plane, then we have:

$$\frac{|\mathbf{f_s}|}{|-\mathbf{n}|} = \frac{y}{x} \tag{1}$$

From proportion (1), we would like to be able to determine $|\mathbf{f_s}|$. Although y and x can be easily measured, $|-\mathbf{n}|$ cannot. However, looking back at figure (b), we note that $\triangle ADE$ is a right triangle, so that the Pythagorean theorem gives $|\mathbf{f_s}|^2 + |-\mathbf{n}|^2 = |\mathbf{w}|^2$, or $|-\mathbf{n}| = \sqrt{|\mathbf{w}|^2 - |\mathbf{f_s}|^2}$. Since $|\mathbf{w}|$ can be measured (that is, since we can find the weight of the object), we will use the proportion

$$\frac{|\mathbf{f_s}|}{\sqrt{|\mathbf{w}|^2 - |\mathbf{f_s}|^2}} = \frac{y}{x} \tag{2}$$

instead of proportion (1).

2. Show that proportion (2), when solved for $|\mathbf{f_s}|$, gives $|\mathbf{f_s}| = \dfrac{y\,|\mathbf{w}|}{\sqrt{x^2 + y^2}}$.

3. Suppose you place an object at one end of a smooth board or other flat surface and slowly raise that end. The magnitude of the static-friction force increases until it reaches its maximum value at the instant before the object finally begins to slide. Perform this experiment and use Exercise 2 to determine the maximum value of $|\mathbf{f_s}|$ for an object and a plane of your choosing. (*Note:* You will need a ruler to measure the rise and run of the plane, and a scale to measure the weight of the object.)

ADVANCED MATHEMATICS
Activities Book

A Journey into Four-Dimensional Space
(For use with Section 12-5)

The Hypercube

Since we perceive the world in three dimensions, we may assume that three is the practical limit to the number of dimensions in geometry. However, if we can represent points in the plane as ordered pairs and points in three-dimensional space as ordered triples, what prevents us from considering ordered quadruples? The fact that we cannot see a four-dimensional geometric world does not mean that it doesn't exist as a mathematical entity. As a matter of fact, we *can* see "shadows" of this four-dimensional world. Here's how:

Draw a point, a zero-dimensional object.

Slide the point one unit; the path you have traced is a segment, a one-dimensional object.

Slide the segment one unit in a perpendicular direction; the endpoints of the segment trace a path that completes a square, a two-dimensional object.

Slide the square in a perpendicular direction and you have a cube, a three-dimensional object. (Note that we recognize the diagram at the right as representing a three-dimensional object even though it is drawn in two dimensions.)

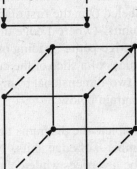

Now slide the cube in a direction perpendicular to all three directions used so far. The problem is that you cannot see where the cube is going. Even so, just slide the diagram of the cube and connect the corresponding vertices of the two cubes. This is the "shadow" of a four-dimensional cube, called a *hypercube*, drawn in two dimensions.

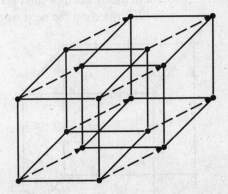

ADVANCED MATHEMATICS
Activities Book

A Journey into Four-Dimensional Space *(Continued)*

1. Copy and complete the table below. (To help you with the hypercube, the number of edges has already been entered in the table. You can obtain this number by reasoning as follows: A hypercube's "shadow" consists of a cube (with 12 edges), a translated copy of the cube (also with 12 edges), and 8 segments connecting the corresponding vertices of the two cubes. Thus, the number of edges of a hypercube is 12 + 12 + 8 = 32.)

	Point	Segment	Square	Cube	Hypercube
Number of vertices	?	?	?	?	?
Number of edges	—	?	?	?	32
Number of faces	—	—	?	?	?
Number of cubes	—	—	—	?	?

Slicing Cubes and Hypercubes

There are a variety of ways to examine the properties of a geometric object. One way is to examine "slices" of the object, thereby reducing by one the number of dimensions being analyzed.

Let's consider parallel planar slices of a cube. If we select a starting vertex, labeled O in the first diagram below, we can move an equal number of "edge units" (where 1 edge unit is one quarter of the length of an edge) along all "edge-paths" leading out from O. Our stopping points then give us the vertices of a slice of the cube. For example, moving 1 edge unit from O gives a two-dimensional triangular slice of the cube, as shown in the second diagram below.

2. Complete the diagrams below and on the next page for each given number n of edge units. Note that whenever you reach one of the cube's vertices while counting edge units, you must complete the count along each of the two edges leading out from that vertex. This is illustrated on the next page for the case $n = 5$.

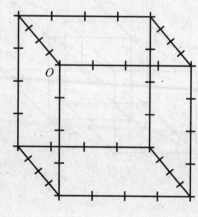

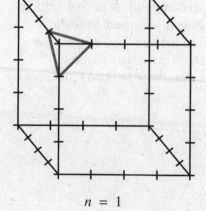

$n = 1$

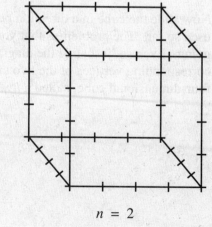

$n = 2$

ADVANCED MATHEMATICS
Activities Book

A Journey into Four-Dimensional Space (Continued)

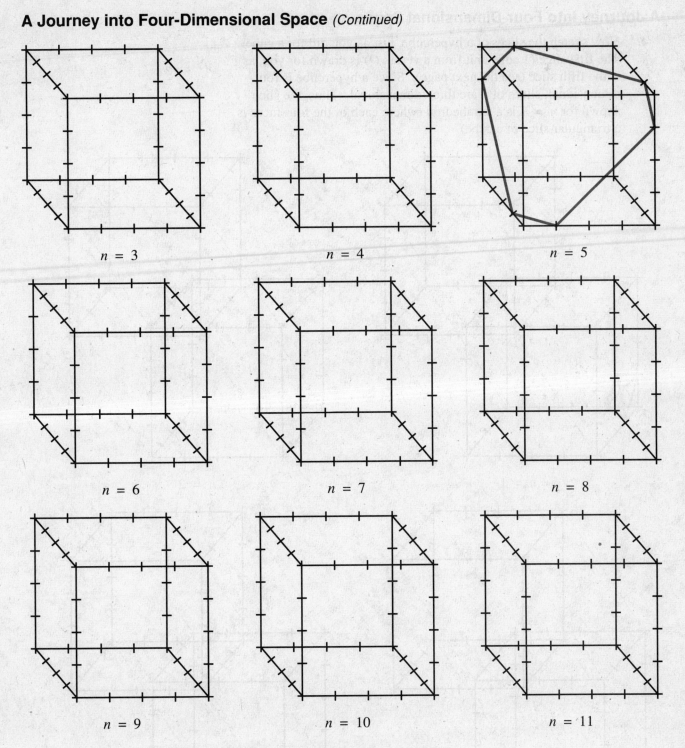

$n = 3$ $n = 4$ $n = 5$

$n = 6$ $n = 7$ $n = 8$

$n = 9$ $n = 10$ $n = 11$

3. Describe any relationships that you see among the slices that you obtained in Exercise 2.

ADVANCED MATHEMATICS
Activities Book

A Journey into Four-Dimensional Space *(Continued)*

4. Now sketch the slices of a hypercube, just as you did for a cube.
    The first slice (1 edge unit from a vertex O) is drawn for you, as
    is the fifth slice (see the next page). Since a hypercube is four-
    dimensional, slices of it are three-dimensional. Thus, the slice
    shown for $n = 1$ is a tetrahedron (where each of the four faces is
    a triangular slice of a cube).

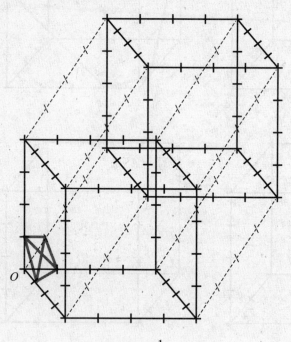

$n = 1$

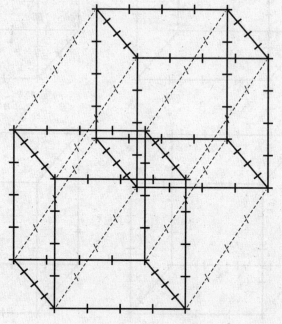

$n = 2$

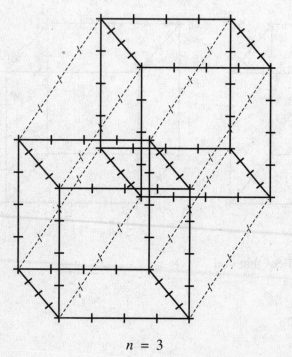

$n = 3$

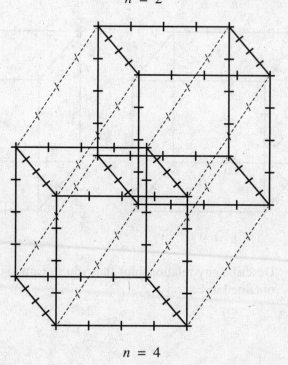

$n = 4$

ADVANCED MATHEMATICS
Activities Book

A Journey into Four-Dimensional Space *(Continued)*

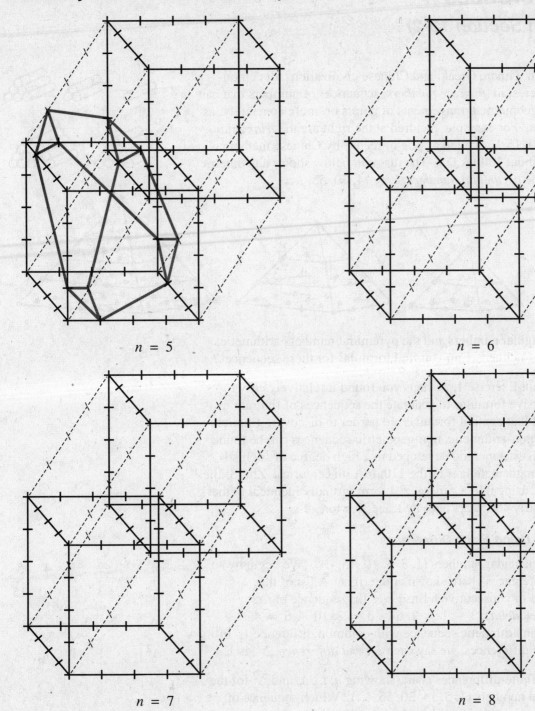

$n = 5$

$n = 6$

$n = 7$

$n = 8$

5.   In Exercise 4, if you were to draw the slice for $n = 9$, to which slice
     already drawn would it be congruent? What about $n = 12$? What
     about $n = 15$?

35

Finite Differences
(For use with Section 13-2)

Ancient Babylonian, Hindu, Greek, and Chinese civilizations all demon-strated an early interest in *figurate numbers*, sequences of numbers that can be represented by geometric arrangements of points or, more concretely, as stackings of objects. For example, pictured at the right are the *triangular numbers*, 1, 3, 6, 10, 15, ..., called a "pile of reeds" by Chinese mathema-tician Zhū Shìjíe (about 1300 A.D.). The diagram below shows a geometric representation of the *pyramidal numbers*, 1, 5, 14, 30, 55, ...

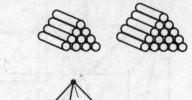

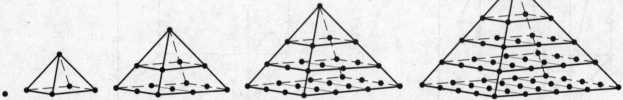

1. Are the triangular numbers and the pyramidal numbers arithmetic, geometric, or neither? Can you find formulas for these sequences?

   In thinking about Exercise 1, perhaps you found it relatively easy to come up with recursive formulas to generate the sequences of figurate numbers, but found that explicit formulas are harder to discover. Explicit formulas for many non-arithmetic, non-geometric sequences can be found using *finite differences*, a method developed to a high degree of sophisti-cation by Chinese mathematicians of the 11th to 13th centuries. Zhū Shìjíe refined the method, using it in a generalized form virtually identical to that given in Europe nearly 400 years later by Isaac Newton.

Finding Formulas Using Finite Differences

First consider the triangular numbers (1, 3, 6, 10, 15, ...). We begin by creating a finite-differences chart, shown at the right. A list of the differences for pairs of consecutive terms gives the sequence of *first differences*, Δ (Greek *delta*): $3 - 1 = 2, 6 - 3 = 3, 10 - 6 = 4$, $15 - 10 = 5, ...$, an arithmetic sequence with common difference 1. In the context of finite differences, we say each *second difference*, Δ^2, is 1.

n	1	2	3	4	5
t_n	1	3	6	10	15
Δ		2	3	4	5
Δ^2			1	1	1

2. a. Create a finite-differences chart, showing n, t_n, Δ, and Δ^2 for the pyramidal numbers (1, 5, 14, 30, 55, ...). Which sequence of differences is arithmetic?

   b. Add a row to your chart for *third differences* (Δ^3).

3. Create a finite-differences chart for each of the following sequences, stopping when the sequence of differences becomes constant.

   a. 1, 5, 12, 22, 35, ...   b. 3, 4, 13, 36, 79, ...   c. −4, 0, 10, 26, 48, ...

Finite Differences (Continued)

The following theorem is stated without proof.

Theorem	If the nth differences of a sequence are constant, then an explicit formula for the sequence is a polynomial of degree n.

According to the theorem, the triangular numbers, with constant second differences, will have a second-degree formula, $t_n = an^2 + bn + c$. A general finite-differences chart for t_n is shown below.

n	1	2	3	4	5
t_n	$a + b + c$	$4a + 2b + c$	$9a + 3b + c$	$16a + 4b + c$	$25a + 5b + c$
Δ		$3a + b$	$5a + b$	?	?
Δ^2		$2a$	?	?	

4. Complete the finite-differences chart for $t_n = an^2 + bn + c$.

   To find a, b, and c, we equate the first expression in each row of the chart above with the number that appears in the corresponding position in the chart for the triangular numbers on the previous page:

$$a + b + c = 1, \quad 3a + b = 2, \quad \text{and} \quad 2a = 1$$

Solving for a, b, and c gives $a = \frac{1}{2}$, $b = \frac{1}{2}$, and $c = 0$; therefore, the

formula for the triangular numbers is $t_n = \frac{1}{2}n^2 + \frac{1}{2}n$, or $t_n = \frac{n(n + 1)}{2}$.

5. Refer back to the illustration of Zhū Shìjíe's "pile of reeds." How many reeds are in a pile 25 layers deep?

6. a. The pyramidal numbers, whose third differences are constant, will have a third-degree formula, $t_n = an^3 + bn^2 + cn + d$. Create a general finite-differences chart for t_n.

   b. Using your charts from Exercise 2 and part (a) of this exercise, solve for a, b, c, and d. Then write an explicit formula for the pyramidal numbers.

7. Find an explicit formula for each of the sequences from Exercise 3.

8. In his book *Precious Mirror of the Four Elements*, Zhū Shìjíe found an explicit formula for the following sequence:

$$3^3, 3^3 + 4^3, 3^3 + 4^3 + 5^3, 3^3 + 4^3 + 5^3 + 6^3, \ldots$$

   a. Using two more terms in addition to those given above, create a finite-differences chart for Zhū Shìjíe's sequence.

   b. An explicit formula for this sequence has what degree?

ADVANCED MATHEMATICS
Activities Book

An Introduction to Cryptology
(For use with Section 14-3)

Modular Arithmetic

The study of secret codes is known as *cryptology*. The art of encipherment, or writing codes, is called *cryptography*, and the science of decipherment, or code cracking, is *cryptanalysis*. Here we concentrate on the cryptographer's dilemma: how to create a procedure for encoding messages that is fairly easy to use but difficult to crack.

First consider a simple technique for encipherment, shown below. The first line of characters lists the 26 letters of the alphabet and 3 punctuation marks. The second line shows the first line shifted four characters to the left (with the first four characters cycling to the end of the line). Thus, "A" becomes encoded as "E," "B" as "F," and so on. Because this encipherment technique was used by Julius Caesar, it is sometimes called a Caesar shift.

Plain text	A	B	C	D	E	F	G	H	I	J	K	L	M	N	O	P	Q	R	S	T	U	V	W	X	Y	Z	.	,	?
Cipher text	E	F	G	H	I	J	K	L	M	N	O	P	Q	R	S	T	U	V	W	X	Y	Z	.	,	?	A	B	C	D

1. Use the key above to encode this message:
   I CAME, I SAW, I CONQUERED.

2. Use the key above to decode this message:
   FI.EVIXLIMHIWB

To make the discussion of encoding and decoding more mathematical, let us uniquely assign each whole number from 0 to 28 to a letter of the alphabet or a punctuation mark, as shown in the first two rows of the table below. Then a Caesar shift of four characters to the left, as discussed above, merely involves adding 4 to the value of a character and subtracting 29 if the sum exceeds 28. Thus, the character "Z," which has a value of 25, becomes encoded as $(25 + 4) - 29 = 0$, or "A." Simple cipher wheels, like the one shown at the right, use this mathematical technique, called *modular* (or *clock*) arithmetic.

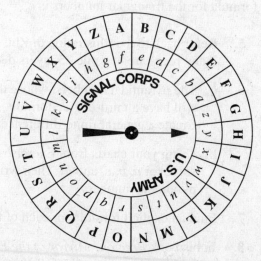

Plain text	A	B	C	D	E	F	G	H	I	J	K	L	M	N	O	P	Q	R	S	T	U	V	W	X	Y	Z	.	,	?
Value	0	1	2	3	4	5	6	7	8	9	10	11	12	13	14	15	16	17	18	19	20	21	22	23	24	25	26	27	28
Encoded value	4	5	6	7	8	9	10	11	12	13	14	15	16	17	18	19	20	21	22	23	24	25	26	27	28	0	1	2	3
Cipher text	E	F	G	H	I	J	K	L	M	N	O	P	Q	R	S	T	U	V	W	X	Y	Z	.	,	?	A	B	C	D

An Introduction to Cryptology *(Continued)*

3. Suppose an encipherment code multiplies each character value by 2 and then subtracts 29 if the product exceeds 28. For example, the character "U," which has a value of 20, becomes encoded as $2 \cdot 20 - 29 = 11$, or "L." Create a table like the one on the preceding page for this encipherment code.

So far we have used 29 characters (with values ranging from 0 to 28). Suppose we now use only the 26 letters of the alphabet (with values ranging from 0 to 25). When encoding these characters, we will subtract 26 instead of 29 when results become too large. Mathematically speaking, we say that we are using a "modulus 26" system instead of a "modulus 29" system.

4. a. Repeat Exercise 3, this time dropping off the last three columns (for encoding the punctuation marks) and using a modulus 26 system. For example, the character "U," which has a value of 20, now becomes encoded as $2 \cdot 20 - 26 = 14$, or "O."

   b. What problem do you see with the encipherment code in part (a)?

   c. Try using 3 as a multiplier instead of 2. (*Note*: You will need to subtract 26 *twice* when encoding the letters S through Z.) Has the problem in part (b) been eliminated?

   d. Based on parts (b) and (c), what conclusion can you draw about the modulus and the multiplier? Use other multipliers to confirm.

5. Mathematically describe the encipherment code used in the cipher wheel shown on the preceding page. (Note that the letters of the alphabet have been reversed as well as shifted.)

6. Find a way to decipher the code described in Exercise 3. (*Hint*: Recall that dividing by a nonzero number is equivalent to multiplying by the number's reciprocal. Also recall that the product of a nonzero number and its reciprocal is 1. In Exercise 3, the multiplier is 2. What, then, is the reciprocal of 2 in a modulus 29 system? That is, for what number x does $2x - 29 = 1$?)

Digraphic Ciphers

Although we have solved half of the cryptographer's dilemma (namely, determining an encipherment technique that is fairly easy to use), we have a very serious problem, that of letter frequency. Certain letters in the English language occur with fairly predictable frequency. Thus, if a few letters of an encoded message can be determined, the message may be decipherable.

One method of scrambling letters is to use a *digraphic cipher*. This involves selecting a 2×2 matrix that has an inverse. For example, at the top of the next page we use the matrix $\begin{bmatrix} 2 & -1 \\ -3 & 4 \end{bmatrix}$ and the table at the bottom of the preceding page to encode the message "NEED HELP" as "WFGADWXT" (with each "E" encoded differently).

ADVANCED MATHEMATICS
Activities Book

An Introduction to Cryptography (Continued)

$$\begin{bmatrix} 2 & -1 \\ -3 & 4 \end{bmatrix}\begin{bmatrix} N & E \\ E & D \end{bmatrix} \rightarrow \begin{bmatrix} 2 & -1 \\ -3 & 4 \end{bmatrix}\begin{bmatrix} 13 & 4 \\ 4 & 3 \end{bmatrix} = \begin{bmatrix} 22 & 5 \\ -23 & 0 \end{bmatrix} \rightarrow \begin{bmatrix} 22 & 5 \\ 6 & 0 \end{bmatrix} \rightarrow \begin{bmatrix} W & F \\ G & A \end{bmatrix}$$

$$\begin{bmatrix} 2 & -1 \\ -3 & 4 \end{bmatrix}\begin{bmatrix} H & E \\ L & P \end{bmatrix} \rightarrow \begin{bmatrix} 2 & -1 \\ -3 & 4 \end{bmatrix}\begin{bmatrix} 7 & 4 \\ 11 & 15 \end{bmatrix} = \begin{bmatrix} 3 & -7 \\ 23 & 48 \end{bmatrix} \rightarrow \begin{bmatrix} 3 & 22 \\ 23 & 19 \end{bmatrix} \rightarrow \begin{bmatrix} D & W \\ X & T \end{bmatrix}$$

Note that when an element of a matrix product is *not* between 0 and 28 (inclusive), we add or subtract a multiple of 29 to obtain a value that *is* between 0 and 28 (inclusive). For example, when "NEED" is encoded, the element -23 is expressed as the equivalent value in the modulus 29 system: $-23 + 29 = 6$.

7. Make up your own message and encode it using $\begin{bmatrix} 3 & -4 \\ 5 & -2 \end{bmatrix}$.

We now face the problem of decoding a message that has been encoded by digraphic cipher. To undo what the encipherment matrix has done, we need to find the inverse of the matrix. (Bear in mind, however, that we are working in a modulus 29 system.) In general, the inverse of the matrix $\begin{bmatrix} a & b \\ c & d \end{bmatrix}$ is $D^{-1}\begin{bmatrix} d & -b \\ -c & a \end{bmatrix}$, where D^{-1} is the multiplicative inverse of the determinant of the matrix. For example, the determinant of $\begin{bmatrix} 2 & -1 \\ -3 & 4 \end{bmatrix}$ is $2(4) - (-3)(-1) = 5$. In a modulus 29 system, the multiplicative inverse of 5 is 6, because $5 \cdot 6 - 29 = 1$ (see the hint for Exercise 6). Thus, the inverse of $\begin{bmatrix} 2 & -1 \\ -3 & 4 \end{bmatrix}$ is $6\begin{bmatrix} 4 & 1 \\ 3 & 2 \end{bmatrix} = \begin{bmatrix} 24 & 6 \\ 18 & 12 \end{bmatrix}$.

8. Show how to decode the message "WFGADWXT" using $\begin{bmatrix} 24 & 6 \\ 18 & 12 \end{bmatrix}$.

9. Find the inverse of the matrix in Exercise 7 and confirm that it decodes your encoded message.

Extensions

For someone experienced in cryptanalysis, digraphic ciphers are not too difficult to break. You can increase the complexity of the code by using trigraphic ciphers and 3 × 3 matrices, or by using keywords that allow you to use different matrices for the same message. Also, you might enjoy writing a computer program that encodes and decodes messages for you.

For further investigation see:

Gardner, Martin. *Penrose Tiles to Trapdoor Ciphers.* New York: W. H. Freeman, 1989.

Peck, Lyman C. *Secret Codes, Remainder Arithmetic, and Matrices.* Reston, VA: NCTM, 1961.

Sinkov, Abraham. *Elementary Cryptanalysis: A Mathematical Approach.* New York: Random House, 1968.

ADVANCED MATHEMATICS
Activities Book

Derangements: Nothing In Its Proper Place
(For use with Section 15-3)

Using the Inclusion-Exclusion Principle to Count Derangements

If you were to put a left shoe on your right foot and a right shoe on your left foot, you would have what mathematicians call (fittingly enough) a *derangement* of the shoes. In general, if a set of objects has some given or "natural" order, then any permutation in which no object is in its proper position is a derangement of the objects. For example, the first three letters of the alphabet have the standard order ABC (where A is in the first position, B in the second, and C in the third), so BCA is a derangement of these letters, but BAC is not (because C is still in the third position).

1. List all the possible derangements of ABC.

2. List all the possible derangements of 1234.

From the discussion and exercises so far, we have seen that only 1 derangement is possible for 2 objects, 2 derangements are possible for 3 objects, and 9 derangements are possible for 4 objects. The obvious question is: How many derangements are possible for n objects?

One way to begin answering the question is to use the inclusion-exclusion principle (see page 566 of the text) and its extensions. For example, in order to count the derangements of ABC, let us define the following sets:

P_A = the set of permutations of ABC in which A is in the first position
P_B = the set of permutations of ABC in which B is in the second position
P_C = the set of permutations of ABC in which C is in the third position

An extension of the inclusion-exclusion principle to these three sets states:

For sets P_A, P_B, and P_C,
$$n(P_A \cup P_B \cup P_C) = [n(P_A) + n(P_B) + n(P_C)] -$$
$$[n(P_A \cap P_B) + n(P_A \cap P_C) + n(P_B \cap P_C)] +$$
$$n(P_A \cap P_B \cap P_C).$$

The Venn diagram at the right shows the sets P_A, P_B, and P_C with their elements. Note that the set $P_A \cup P_B \cup P_C$ contains the permutations of ABC that are *not* derangements. Using the inclusion-exclusion principle stated above, we have:

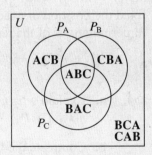

$$n(P_A \cup P_B \cup P_C) = [2 + 2 + 2] - [1 + 1 + 1] + 1$$
$$= 6 - 3 + 1 = 4$$

Then, using the complement principle (see page 574 of the text), we know that the number of derangements of ABC is just the number of *possible* permutations minus the number of permutations that are *not* derangements; that is,

$$n(\text{derangements}) = 3! - n(P_A \cup P_B \cup P_C) = 6 - 4 = 2.$$

ADVANCED MATHEMATICS
Activities Book

Derangements: Nothing In Its Place *(Continued)*

3. To count the number of derangements of 1234, consider these sets:

P_1 = the set of permutations of 1234 in which 1 is in the first position
P_2 = the set of permutations of 1234 in which 2 is in the second position
P_3 = the set of permutations of 1234 in which 3 is in the third position
P_4 = the set of permutations of 1234 in which 4 is in the fourth position

When extended to four sets, the inclusion-exclusion principle states:

For sets P_1, P_2, P_3, and P_4,

$$n(P_1 \cup P_2 \cup P_3 \cup P_4) = [n(P_1) + n(P_2) + n(P_3) + n(P_4)] -$$
$$[n(P_1 \cap P_2) + n(P_1 \cap P_3) + n(P_1 \cap P_4) +$$
$$n(P_2 \cap P_3) + n(P_2 \cap P_4) + n(P_3 \cap P_4)] +$$
$$[n(P_1 \cap P_2 \cap P_3) + n(P_1 \cap P_2 \cap P_4) +$$
$$n(P_1 \cap P_3 \cap P_4) + n(P_2 \cap P_3 \cap P_4)] -$$
$$n(P_1 \cap P_2 \cap P_3 \cap P_4).$$

a. Find $n(P_1 \cup P_2 \cup P_3 \cup P_4)$, the number of permutations of 1234 that are *not* derangements. (*Note*: Use combinatorial reasoning rather than a Venn diagram. For example, think of the possible ways of using the digits 1, 2, 3, and 4 to fill four boxes:

□ □ □ □

To find, say, $n(P_1 \cap P_2)$, you would reason that the first box can be filled in only 1 way (since P_1 requires that we put 1 in the first position), the second box can be filled in only 1 way (since P_2 requires that we put 2 in the second position), the third box can be filled in 2 ways (with either 3 or 4), and the fourth box can be filled in only 1 way (with whatever digit is left); therefore, $n(P_1 \cap P_2) = 1 \cdot 1 \cdot 2 \cdot 1 = 2$.)

b. Use the result of part (a) to find the number of derangements of 1234. Check this number against your list from Exercise 2.

In completing part (a) of Exercise 3, you may have noticed that all the addends inside each pair of square brackets are equal. For example, $n(P_1) = n(P_2) = n(P_3) = n(P_4)$, because in each case we have chosen and fixed the position of exactly 1 of the 4 digits and then considered the 3! permutations of the remaining 3 digits; thus,

$$n(P_1) + n(P_2) + n(P_3) + n(P_4) = 3! + 3! + 3! + 3!$$
$$= {}_4C_1 \cdot 3! = 4 \cdot 6 = 24.$$

4. a. Explain why $n(P_1 \cap P_2) + n(P_1 \cap P_3) + n(P_1 \cap P_4) + n(P_2 \cap P_3) + n(P_2 \cap P_4) + n(P_3 \cap P_4) = {}_4C_2 \cdot 2!$.

b. Complete the following equation for finding the number of permutations of 1234 that are not derangements:

$$n(P_1 \cup P_2 \cup P_3 \cup P_4) = {}_4C_1 \cdot 3! - {}_4C_2 \cdot 2! + \underline{\ ?\ } - \underline{\ ?\ }$$

c. Using your answer to part (b), write an equation for finding the number of derangements of 1234.

Derangements: Nothing In Its Place *(Continued)*

Now, for the derangements of 12345, our previous work suggests:

n(derangements) $= n$(permutations) $- n$(nonderangements)

$$= 5! - [\,_5C_1 \cdot 4! - \,_5C_2 \cdot 3! + \,_5C_3 \cdot 2! - \,_5C_4 \cdot 1! + \,_5C_5 \cdot 0!\,]$$

Each term inside the square brackets can be simplified if we replace $_nC_r$

with $\dfrac{n!}{r!\,(n-r)!}$ (see page 578 of the text):

$$n\text{(derangements)} = 5! - \left[\frac{5!}{1!\,4!} \cdot 4! - \frac{5!}{2!\,3!} \cdot 3! + \frac{5!}{3!\,2!} \cdot 2! - \frac{5!}{4!\,1!} \cdot 1! + \frac{5!}{5!\,0!} \cdot 0!\right]$$

$$= 5! - \left[\frac{5!}{1!} - \frac{5!}{2!} + \frac{5!}{3!} - \frac{5!}{4!} + \frac{5!}{5!}\right] = 5! - 5!\left[\frac{1}{1!} - \frac{1}{2!} + \frac{1}{3!} - \frac{1}{4!} + \frac{1}{5!}\right]$$

$$= 5!\left[1 - \frac{1}{1!} + \frac{1}{2!} - \frac{1}{3!} + \frac{1}{4!} - \frac{1}{5!}\right]$$

5. Use the equation above to find the number of derangements of 12345.

6. Find the number of derangements of ABCDEF.

If we symbolize the number of derangements of n objects by d_n, then a general (explicit) formula for d_n is

$$d_n = n!\left[1 - \frac{1}{1!} + \frac{1}{2!} - \frac{1}{3!} + \cdots \pm \frac{1}{n!}\right]$$

where the plus and minus signs alternate throughout the square brackets. In Chapter 19, you will learn that as the value of n increases, the value of the expression inside the square brackets approaches $\dfrac{1}{e}$. Thus, $d_n \approx \dfrac{n!}{e}$.

A Recursive Approach to Counting Derangements

Now that we have found an explicit formula for d_n, let us try to find a recursive formula. In the table at the right, notice that each value of d_n is either 1 more or 1 less than n times the value of d_{n-1}. That is, $d_2 = 2 \cdot d_1 + 1, d_3 = 3 \cdot d_2 - 1, d_4 = 4 \cdot d_3 + 1$, and so on. This suggests the following recursive definition:

$$d_n = \begin{cases} 0 & \text{if } n = 1 \\ n \cdot d_{n-1} + (-1)^n & \text{if } n > 1 \end{cases}$$

n	d_n
1	0
2	1
3	2
4	9
5	44
6	265

7. Find d_7 by using **(a)** the explicit formula for d_n and **(b)** the recursive formula for d_n.

8. Use the table above to find a recursive formula for d_n that involves both d_{n-1} and d_{n-2}.

9. **a.** Using a recursive formula for d_n, write a computer program that computes and prints the value of d_n for a given value of n.

   b. Suppose you want to devise a secret code that uniquely replaces each letter of the alphabet with a different letter. Use the program from part (a) to determine how many secret codes are possible.

ADVANCED MATHEMATICS
Activities Book

Assessing Risk
(For use with Section 16-1)

Probabilities are easily misunderstood, misinterpreted, and misused, especially when people are discussing risk. It is important for everyone to have a clear idea of what probabilities really mean and what they imply in various situations.

1. a. Before going to an outdoor ball game, you hear that there is a 90% chance of rain. Because taking a poncho with you is inconvenient, you decide to go without it. Is doing so worth the risk?

    b. Would it be acceptable to have a 90% chance of getting home safely after the game? Explain the difference between your answer to this question and your answer to the question in part (a).

2. a. Suppose you are given the choice between a sure gain of $10,000 and a $\frac{2}{3}$ chance of a $15,000 gain with a $\frac{1}{3}$ chance of a $0 gain. Which would you choose?

    b. Repeat part (a), but this time substitute "loss" for "gain."

    c. Were your choices in parts (a) and (b) consistent? (For example, did you choose the "sure thing" both times?) If not, how do you reconcile your choices?

    d. Check with your classmates about their choices in parts (a) and (b). Can you draw any general conclusion regarding how people feel about risk when a gain is involved? when a loss is involved?

3. a. From your own point of view, rank in decreasing order of safety the following major forms of transportation in the U.S.: airplanes, automobiles, buses, and trains.

    b. Consult an almanac or other authoritative source to find whatever information you can about the relative safety of the forms of transportation listed in part (a). Does your answer to part (a) agree with your research? If not, try to explain any discrepancies.

The Fall of Skylab

In the summer of 1979, newspapers and newscasts were filled with stories about the fall of *Skylab*, a large orbiting space laboratory launched in 1973. (An overhead view of *Skylab* is shown at the right.) People were told that as *Skylab* reentered Earth's atmosphere, it would disintegrate, showering debris over Earth's surface. People were naturally concerned that they might get hit by a piece of *Skylab*.

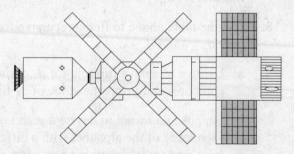

ADVANCED MATHEMATICS
Activities Book

Assessing Risk *(Continued)*

4. **a.** The radius of Earth is about 6400 km. Use the formula for the surface area of a sphere, $A = 4\pi r^2$, to find the surface area of Earth. Give the answer in square kilometers, and then convert it to square meters.

    b. Suppose a piece of *Skylab* was the size of a refrigerator, with a cross section of about 2 m². If this piece randomly fell to Earth, use part (a) to approximate the probability that it would land at a particular location occupied by some person.

    c. Interpret the probability in part (b). Was there much risk of someone being hit? What if 10 or even 100 refrigerator-sized pieces fell to Earth?

5. How do the news media affect people's *perception* of risk? What do you think can or should be done by the news media to put risk in its proper perspective?

Making Decisions

At what point do the risks of medication outweigh the benefits? How safe does a safety helmet have to be? Should people be required by law to take risk-reducing actions—such as using seat belts when driving—even when many find the actions inconvenient or uncomfortable? Such questions are politically and emotionally charged, yet we need to be informed and reasonable when attempting to answer them.

Consider the following situation: A recycling plant was to be constructed near a large city. A computer study, simulating the operation of the plant, suggested that running the plant would increase the local cancer rate by 0.12 per million people. Construction of the plant was stopped because of this study.

6. **a.** Express 0.12 per million as a decimal. What does this decimal represent?

    b. The overall probability that any individual in this country will develop cancer is about 0.2. How does your knowledge of this probability affect the significance of the 0.12-per-million figure?

    c. Comment on the reasonableness of the decision to stop construction of the recycling plant.

    d. What else would you like to know about the plant and about the computer study?

7. Investigate and write about a situation where there is some level of acceptable risk. Be sure to discuss how great the risk is, and to explain why the risk is acceptable.

ADVANCED MATHEMATICS
Activities Book

Factorial Designs
(For use with Section 17-5)

Factorial designs of statistical experiments are used to discover relationships between two or more factors and some variable of interest. Measured changes in the variable can be explained not only by the factors' separate influences (called *main effects*), but also by the factors' combined influences (called *interactions*).

Let's investigate a simple example. In 1985, the average amount of trash produced per person per day in the United States was 3.49 lb. Is there any connection between people's attitudes and the amount of trash they produce? Suppose that a group of people are classified according to two factors: their yes-no opinions of whether they think that recycling is worth the cost and effort, and whether they consider themselves to be liberal, moderate, or conservative in their overall viewpoints. A classification like this, with 2 possible opinions and 3 possible viewpoints, is an example of a 2 × 3 factorial design. Now, suppose that five people from each opinion-viewpoint combination are asked to monitor how many pounds of trash they produce in a day. The results of this experiment are given below.

Opinion	Viewpoint	Weight of trash (in lb)				
yes	liberal	3.2	2.9	2.8	3.1	3.0
yes	moderate	3.5	3.2	3.0	3.2	3.1
yes	conservative	3.0	3.1	2.8	3.2	3.2
no	liberal	3.3	3.1	3.5	3.0	3.4
no	moderate	3.4	3.6	3.3	3.0	3.5
no	conservative	3.2	3.4	3.1	3.3	3.2

1. To see the effects of each factor for this particular set of data, copy and complete the following table of means. (Note that a column mean is based on a particular viewpoint, regardless of opinion, and that a row mean is based on a particular opinion, regardless of viewpoint. For example, the column mean for "liberal," 3.13, is the mean of the 10 numbers in the first and fourth rows of the table above.)

		Viewpoint			Row means
		liberal	moderate	conservative	
Opinion	yes	3.00	?	?	?
	no	3.26	?	?	?
Column means		3.13	?	?	

Factorial Designs (Continued)

2. Compare the row means in Exercise 1. Is there a difference in the mean weight of trash between a "yes" and a "no" opinion? Why is this comparison a measure of the main effect of opinion?

3. Compare the column means. Does the main effect of viewpoint seem to make a difference in the amount of trash produced? Which viewpoint(s), if any, seem to produce the least amount of trash?

4. a. To study interaction, you'll need to calculate the differences in means between opinions. Copy and complete the table below.

		Viewpoint		
		liberal	moderate	conservative
Opinion	yes	3.00	?	?
	no	3.26	?	?
Differences		−0.26	?	?

   b. If the mean differences between opinions for each viewpoint were the same, then the interaction effect would be 0. In other words, any differences between people with different opinions would not appear to depend on the viewpoints of those people. Does there seem to be any opinion-by-viewpoint interaction in this experiment?

5. One way of displaying interaction information is to graph the mean weight of trash versus viewpoints by opinion. Two sample graphs (not based on the given data) are shown below.

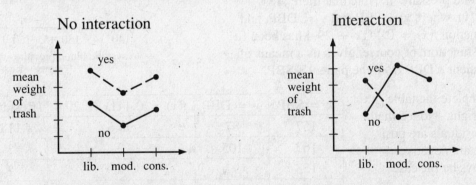

   a. Explain why the graphs for "yes" and "no" opinions are equidistant if there is no interaction, while the distances between the graphs vary from viewpoint to viewpoint if there is an interaction.

   b. Draw a similar graph for the given data, and use it to explain any opinion-by-viewpoint interaction.

6. If you were to reproduce the given experiment, do you think your results would be almost the same? Try it!

Comparing Residuals
(For use with Section 18-4)

Residual Errors and the MSE

Look at the scatter plot of the income-versus-education data on page 683 of the text. As you can see, even though the data points are *essentially* linear, no line can be found that passes through every point. This is due to the fact that the data contain "noise," which is attributable to inaccuracies of measurement, the influences of variables not considered or accounted for, and so on. Thus, no matter what line we try to fit to the data, we can expect some of the data points to lie above the line and some to lie below it.

To better understand how well a particular curve $y = f(x)$ fits a set of paired data (x_1, y_1), (x_2, y_2), ..., (x_n, y_n), let us consider the vertical displacement to each data point (x_i, y_i) from the corresponding point $(x_i, f(x_i))$ on the curve. This displacement, called the *residual error*, is given by

$$e_i = y_i - f(x_i).$$

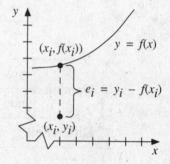

1. In the graph shown at the right, is e_i positive or negative?

2. Consider the beating of your heart. As you would expect, the pressure in your arteries when your heart beats is greater than the pressure when your heart is between beats. Thus, when your blood pressure is taken, you are told two numbers: your systolic blood pressure (SBP) for when your heart contracts, and your diastolic blood pressure (DBP) for when your heart rests. At the right is a scatter plot of blood-pressure data for a patient with moderate hypertension ("high blood pressure"). Note that there are 10 data points (x, y), where $x = $ SBP and $y = $ DBP, and that the linear function $f(x) = 0.441x + 29.4$ has been fit to the data. This function, of course, gives us a means of estimating the patient's DBP from the patient's SBP.

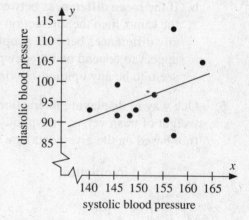

a. Copy and complete the table shown at the right. Notice that some of the residuals are positive and some are negative. Will this always be the case?

b. To determine how well the graph of f fits the data, we need to combine the residuals to get a single number that indicates their overall magnitude. Suppose we consider the *mean* of the residuals. Explain why this statistic is inadequate.

$x = $ SBP	$y = $ DBP	$f(x) = 0.441x + 29.4$	Residual
157	87	98.6	−11.6
163	105	?	?
153	97	?	?
157	113	?	?
140	93	?	?
149	93	?	?
148	92	?	?
146	99	?	?
146	92	?	?
156	91	?	?

Comparing Residuals (Continued)

One way of getting around the problem encountered in part (b) of
Exercise 2 is to use the mean of *squared* residual errors (MSE), given by:

$$\text{MSE} = \frac{\sum\limits_{i=1}^{n} e_i^2}{n} = \frac{\sum\limits_{i=1}^{n} (y_i - f(x_i))^2}{n}$$

Notice the similarity between the formula for MSE and the one for variance
given on page 654 of the text.

3. Calculate the MSE for the blood-pressure data in Exercise 2. Based
    on how well the graph of *f* appears to fit the data, would you say that
    a statistician might consider the MSE to be high or low?

Using the MSE to Choose the Best Model

Choosing which model from among several that best describes a set of data
can be difficult, particularly when the graph of the data seems slightly
curved. As you'll see, using the MSE can be quite helpful.

Consider the rising cost of health care in the United States. In 1977,
8.5% of the entire gross national product (GNP) was spent on health care.
In 1987, the figure had jumped to 11.1% of GNP. The table and graph
below show the total U.S. health expenditures (in billions of dollars) for
each of the years from 1977 to 1987.

x = years (since 1900)	y = U.S. health expenditures (in billions of dollars)
77	169.9
78	189.6
79	214.7
80	248.1
81	287.0
82	323.6
83	357.2
84	388.5
85	419.0
86	455.7
87	500.3

4. **a.** Fit a line to the health-expenditure data. Then calculate the
    residuals and the MSE.

    b. Using a computer or graphing calculator, graph the data with the
    line from part (a). Do you think that the MSE from part (a)
    would be considered high or low?

Comparing Residuals (Continued)

5. The MSE from part (a) of Exercise 4 is about the same as the MSE from Exercise 3. Even so, a line fits the blood-pressure data rather poorly, while a line fits the health-expenditure data rather well. Why don't the two MSE's reflect this fact?

6. **a.** Fit an exponential curve to the health-expenditure data. Then calculate the residuals and the MSE.

   b. Using a computer or graphing calculator, graph the data with the exponential curve from part (a). Can you tell simply from the graph whether the exponential curve provides a better fit than the the line in Exercise 4?

7. Why is it acceptable to compare the MSE's from part (a) of Exercises 4 and 6? Based on the MSE's, which curve—the linear or the exponential—seems to fit the health-expenditure data better?

8. **a.** Fit a power curve to the health-expenditure data. Then calculate the residuals and the MSE.

   b. Compare the MSE for the power curve with the MSE's for the exponential and linear curves from part (a) of Exercises 4 and 6. Which of the three curves provides the best fit?

ADVANCED MATHEMATICS
Activities Book

Another Look at Julia Sets

(For use with Chapter 19 Project: Chaos in the Complex Plane)

The Inverse Iteration Method

The Julia set of the function $f(z) = z^2 + c$, where z and c are complex numbers, is the boundary between two sets of points: those whose orbits escape to infinity and those whose orbits converge or cycle in some way. The computer program on page 753 of the text generates a filled-in Julia set for a given value of c by checking the orbits of over 10,000 complex numbers and plotting those whose orbits do not escape to infinity.

Another method of generating a Julia set is the inverse iteration method, which plots the *backward* orbit of some starting point z_0. The backward orbit of z_0 consists of a predecessor of z_0, a predecessor of that predecessor, and so on. For the function $f(z) = z^2 + c$, a predecessor of z_0 is a number z_{-1} such that $f(z_{-1}) = (z_{-1})^2 + c = z_0$, or $z_{-1} = \pm\sqrt{z_0 - c}$. Likewise, a predecessor of z_{-1} is a number z_{-2} such that $f(z_{-2}) = z_{-1}$, or $z_{-2} = \pm\sqrt{z_{-1} - c}$. Note that at each step in the inverse iteration process, we have a choice between taking a positive and a negative square root; the inverse iteration method works best when the choice is made randomly.

Amazingly, the backward orbit of *any* nonzero number z_0 eventually approaches the Julia set of $f(z) = z^2 + c$. The BASIC program below implements the inverse iteration method using $z_0 = 1 + i$. Before running the program, you will need to complete lines 60 and 220.

```
10   LET PI = 3.14159
20   PRINT "REAL PART OF COMPLEX CONSTANT";
30   INPUT CX
40   PRINT "IMAGINARY PART OF COMPLEX CONSTANT";
50   INPUT CY
60                                          (Insert command for a blank graphics screen.)
70   LET X = 1                              (Initialize the starting point, z₀.)
80   LET Y = 1
90   FOR K = 1 TO 5000                      (Do 5000 iterations.)
100  LET X = X - CX                         (Compute z = z₀ - c.)
110  LET Y = Y - CY
120  IF X > 0 THEN LET T = ATN(Y/X)/2       (Compute polar angle of √z; see Section 11-4.)
130  IF X < 0 THEN LET T = (PI + ATN(Y/X))/2
140  IF X = 0 THEN LET T = PI/4
150  LET R = SQR(SQR(X * X + Y * Y))        (Compute absolute value of √z.)
160  IF RND(1) < 0.5 THEN LET R = -R        (Randomly choose between √z and -√z.)
170  LET X = R * COS(T)                     (Convert to rectangular form.)
180  LET Y = R * SIN(T)
190  LET A = X * 25 + 50                    (Convert to screen coordinates.)
200  LET B = 50 - 25 * Y
210  IF K < 10 THEN GOTO 230                (Don't plot the first 10 iterations.)
220                                         (Insert command for plotting (A, B).)
230  NEXT K
240  END
```

Another Look at Julia Sets *(Continued)*

1. Run the program for $c = 0 + 0i$. What do you observe?

2. Run the program for $c = -1.139 + 0.238i$ and compare the result with the filled-in Julia set shown on page 753 of the text.

Julia Sets in Relation to the Mandelbrot Set

Julia sets associated with $f(z) = z^2 + c$ vary greatly in appearance depending on where the constant c is located in relation to the Mandelbrot set, shown at the right. In effect, the Mandelbrot set serves as a "catalogue" of the various Julia sets.

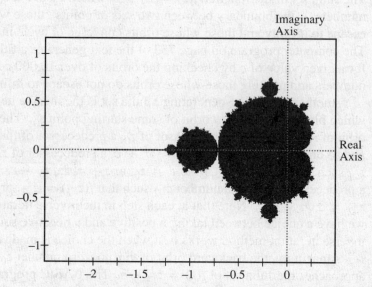

For the values of c given in Exercises 3–8, do the following:

a. Use the Mandelbrot set shown at the right to determine whether c appears to be inside the Mandelbrot set, outside the set, or on the border of the set.

b. Use the program given on the preceding page to obtain the Julia set of $f(z) = z^2 + c$. Then indicate which of the following four categories best describes the Julia set:

   (i) a mostly connected curve that is smooth and encloses some region;

   (ii) a mostly connected curve that has many protrusions and encloses one or more regions;

   (iii) a mostly connected curve that has many squiggles and offshoots but does not enclose some region;

   (iv) disconnected clumps of points.

c. Decide whether the Julia set has point symmetry, line symmetry, or both.

3. $-0.3 + 0i$ 4. $0 + 0.5i$ 5. $-1 + i$

6. $0 + i$ 7. $-1 + 0i$ 8. $0.5 + 0.5i$

9. Try several other complex numbers that are obviously located *inside* the Mandelbrot set and note the appearance of the Julia sets formed. How are the sets alike?

10. Try several other complex numbers that are obviously located *outside* the Mandelbrot set and note the appearance of the Julia sets formed. How are the sets alike?

11. Compare the Julia sets of $f(z) = z^2 + c$ for values of c that are complex conjugates. (For example, try $c = 0.4 + 2i$ and $c = 0.4 - 2i$.)

12. For what type of constant c does the Julia set of $f(z) = z^2 + c$ appear to be symmetric with respect to a horizontal or a vertical line?

ADVANCED MATHEMATICS
Activities Book

Position, Velocity, and Acceleration
(For use with Section 20-4)

In observing the world around us, we see that change is always taking place—in the motion of stars and planets, in the size of populations of living things, and so on. Calculus provides the mathematical means for describing such change.

   Consider a car as it travels down a road. The car's *velocity* is the change in the car's position with respect to time. Similarly, the car's *acceleration* is the change in the car's velocity with respect to time. Position, velocity, and acceleration can all be related through derivatives, as shown in Section 20-4. Let's take a more informal approach to these concepts here, however.

1. **a.** The graph at the right shows the distance that you travel when you drive a car at a constant speed. (Speed is the absolute value of velocity.) Explain how to determine the car's speed from the graph.

    b. How would the graph change if the car is driven at a constant speed that is *slower* than the speed in part (a)?

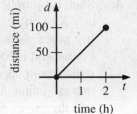

2. Imagine that you are driving from city A to city B. Your distance from city A increases as elapsed time increases, but the *rate* at which the distance increases varies: Although you can proceed rapidly on the open highway, you would travel at a slower speed in the two cities and their surrounding suburbs. Bearing this in mind, complete the graph at the right by drawing a simple broken-line curve that reasonably reflects the way distance from city A increases as time elapses.

3. The graph at the right shows the relationship between distance and time as a teacher drives from her home to the high school at which she teaches. Her route is as follows: She travels down the lane from her home until she comes to an intersection with a road leading to the highway. She turns onto the road, travels down it, and then turns onto the highway. She then proceeds to the second exit, where she gets onto a road leading to the high school. Not far from the school, she stops for a school bus that is picking up students. She then continues down the road and turns onto a driveway leading to the school's parking lot, where she parks her car.

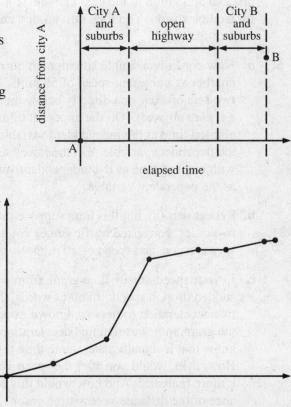

elapsed time

ADVANCED MATHEMATICS
Activities Book

Position, Velocity, and Acceleration *(Continuod)*

3. *(continued)*

a. Label with an "A" the point on the graph where the teacher stops for the school bus. Label with a "B" the point on the graph where the teacher gets on the highway. Label with a "C" the point on the graph where the teacher pulls into the school's driveway.

b. During which period of time is the car's speed the greatest? How does the graph justify your answer?

c. During which period of time is the car's speed the least? How does the graph justify your answer?

4. Sketch a graph, like the one in Exercise 3, representing a trip from city X to city Y, which are connected by an interstate highway. The trip proceeds as follows: Traveling on the highway from city X, your speed is 55 mi/h until you reach the hills near city Y. You then reduce your speed to 35 mi/h because you are stuck behind trucks that are going slowly over the hills. Unfortunately, the distraction that the trucks provide causes you to miss the exit to city Y, so you proceed at 55 mi/h to the next exit and stop at a roadside restaurant for a quick snack. You then turn around and go back at 55 mi/h to the exit for city Y.

5. a. Now consider a simple situation: You're driving from one city to another at a constant speed of 55 mi/h. To illustrate this, draw two sets of axes, one directly below the other (so that the vertical axes are aligned). On the upper set of axes, sketch a graph with elapsed time as the independent variable and distance traveled as the dependent variable. On the lower set of axes, sketch a graph with elapsed time as the independent variable and the car's speed as the dependent variable.

b. Repeat part (a), but this time suppose that halfway between the two cities, congested traffic forces you to drive the rest of the way at a constant speed of 40 mi/h.

c. In your speed-versus-time graph from part (b), you should see a sudden drop in speed. In other words, the car experiences negative acceleration (otherwise known as deceleration). Although the graph indicates that this deceleration is instantaneous, we know that it actually takes some time for the car to decelerate. How, then, would you alter the speed-versus-time graph to make it more realistic? And how would this change affect the appearance of the distance-versus-time graph?

ADVANCED MATHEMATICS
Activities Book

Answers

Using Parabolas to Solve Quadratic Equations, pages 1–2

1. Position the parabola $y = x^2$ so that it opens downward, with its vertex at (3, 1) and its axis of symmetry parallel to the y-axis. **2. a.** (1, −9); 4, −2 **b.** (−3, 2); −4, −2 **c.** (−4, 2); no real roots **3. a.** $y = -(x - 2)^2$; (2, 0); 2 (a double root)

b. $y = 2\left(x + \frac{1}{2}\right)^2 - \frac{9}{2}$; $\left(-\frac{1}{2}, -\frac{9}{2}\right)$; −2, 1

c. $y = -\frac{1}{2}(x - 1)^2 - \frac{5}{2}$; $\left(1, -\frac{5}{2}\right)$; no real roots

4. $k = 0$; k is positive; k is negative. **5.** Position the parabola $y = |a|x^2$ so that it opens upward when $a > 0$ and downward when $a < 0$, the axis of symmetry is parallel to the y-axis, and the x-intercepts of the parabola are the roots of the equation $a(x - h)^2 + k = 0$. **6. a.** (2, −1); (2, −2); (2, 0.5) **b.** (1, −9); (1, −18); (1, 4.5) **c.** (1, −4); (1, −8); (1, 2)

Algorithms and Polynomial Time, pages 3–5

1. a. Trial Divisions Algorithm

M	N	D	F	Q1	Q2
36	24	2	1	18	12
18	12	3	2	9	6
9	6		4	4.5	3
3	2		(12)	3	2

Euclidean Algorithm

M	N	Q	R
36	24	1	12
24	(12)	2	0

b. Euclidean algorithm is more efficient.
2. Trial Divisions Algorithm

```
10  INPUT "LARGER POSITIVE INTEGER:   "; M
20  INPUT "SMALLER POSITIVE INTEGER:   "; N
30  LET D = 2
40  LET F = 1
50  IF D > N THEN GOTO 100
60  LET Q1 = M / D
70  LET Q2 = N / D
80  IF INT (Q1) = Q1 AND INT (Q2) = Q2 THEN
    LET F = F * D: LET M = Q1: LET N = Q2:
    GOTO 50
90  IF INT (Q1) < > Q1 OR INT (Q2) < > Q2
    THEN LET D = D + 1: GOTO 50
100  PRINT "THE GCF IS "; F
110  END
```

Euclidean Algorithm

```
10  INPUT "LARGER POSITIVE INTEGER:   "; M
20  INPUT "SMALLER POSITIVE INTEGER:   "; N
30  LET Q = INT (M / N)
40  LET R = M - Q * N
50  IF R < > 0 THEN LET M = N: LET N = R:
    GOTO 30
60  PRINT "THE GCF IS "; N
70  END
```

3. a. 9 divisions are performed. **b.** 21 and 13, for example **4.** The worst case occurs when either M or N is a prime number; for example, $M = 60$, $N = 13$ requires 12 divisions.

5.

n	1	2	3	4	5	...	10	...	50	...	100
n^2	1	4	9	16	25	...	100	...	2500	...	10,000
2^n	2	4	8	16	32	...	1024	...	1.13×10^{15}	...	1.27×10^{30}

6. a. When n is small, $n^2 \approx 2^n$. **b.** When n is large, the value of 2^n is significantly greater than the value of n^2.
7. a. bin 1: 7, 3, 2; bin 2: 6, 6; bin 3: 4, 3, 3, 2 **b.** bin 1: 6, 4; bin 2: 5, 4; bin 3: 3, 3, 3; bin 4: 2 **c.** bin 1: 6, 4; bin 2: 5, 3, 2; bin 3: 4, 3, 3

Equalizers and Inequalities, pages 6–7

1. a. −12 dB ≤ I ≤ 12 dB **b.** 38 dB ≤ I ≤ 62 dB
2. a. 80 Hz ≤ f ≤ 160 Hz, 160 Hz ≤ f ≤ 320 Hz, 320 Hz ≤ f ≤ 640 Hz, 640 Hz ≤ f ≤ 1280 Hz, 1280 Hz ≤ f ≤ 2560 Hz, 2560 Hz ≤ f ≤ 5120 Hz, 5120 Hz ≤ f ≤ 10,240 Hz, 10,240 Hz ≤ f ≤ 20,480 Hz; 10 octaves **b.** Each frequency shown on the equalizer uniquely falls within one of the 10 octaves of human hearing. **c.** A five-band equalizer would give you less control, because each slider would control 2 octaves. **3.** a lighter band from about 4 kHz to about 15 kHz; 20 Hz ≤ f ≤ 15,000 Hz
4. Answers may vary slightly. **a.** 260 Hz ≤ f ≤ 14,000 Hz; 250, 500, 1 k, 2 k, 4 k, 8 k, 16 k **b.** 60 Hz ≤ f ≤ 8000 Hz; 64, 125, 250, 500, 1 k, 2 k, 4 k, 8 k
c. 80 Hz ≤ f ≤ 1800 Hz; 125, 250, 500, 1 k, 2 k
d. 140 Hz ≤ f ≤ 18,000 Hz; 125, 250, 500, 1 k, 2 k, 4 k, 8 k, 16 k **5.** Answers may vary slightly. **a.** most woodwinds and strings; also cymbals and piano **b.** piano, double bass, tuba, and bassoon **c.** all sounds except bass voice **d.** all sounds except piccolo **6. a.** "Boosting" at 32 Hz and 64 Hz increases the intensity of bass sounds, which usually give the beat in disco music. "Cutting" at 2 kHz and 4 kHz decreases the intensity of vocalists' overtones, which give the vocalists a nasal sound.

Contour Maps, pages 8–9

1. ≈ 3800 ft (above sea level) **2.** Answers will vary.
3. Answers will vary. **4.** Such a path would be indicated by contour lines that are comparatively farther apart than those along other paths. **5.** The contour map would be basically the same, but there would be more or fewer contour lines depending on whether thinner or thicker cardboard was used.

Logarithms and the Slide Rule, pages 10–11

1.

Number	1	10	100
Number written as a power of 10	10^0	10^1	10^2
Exponent of number written as a power of 10	0	1	2

2. $d = \log N$

3.

N	log N	N	log N	N	log N	N	log N
1	0.00	5	0.70	10	1.00	60	1.78
1.5	0.18	6	0.78	20	1.30	70	1.85
2	0.30	7	0.85	30	1.48	80	1.90
3	0.48	8	0.90	40	1.60	90	1.95
4	0.60	9	0.95	50	1.70	100	2.00

ADVANCED MATHEMATICS
Activities Book

4. a.

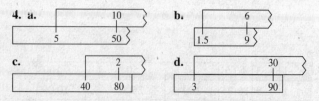

5. One pointer is set to 1 (the beginning of the logarithmic scale), and the other pointer is set to 2. The angle α formed by the pointers is then preserved as the pointers are rotated counterclockwise until the first pointer is at 3. The result of multiplying 2 and 3 is read from the second pointer, which is at 6. To divide 6 by 3, set the pointers at 1 and 3. Preserving the angle β formed by the pointers, rotate them counterclockwise until the second one is at 6. The first pointer gives the quotient, 2.

Conics and Telescopes, pages 12–14

1. a.   **b.**

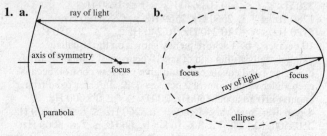

2. a. f/11   **b.** 660 in. or 55 ft

3. a.

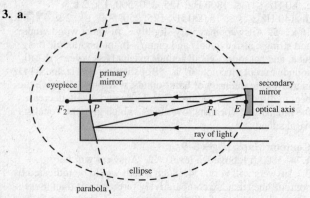

b. 9 in.

4. a.

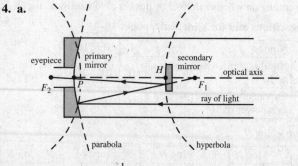

b. 7.2 in.   **5. a.** $x = \frac{1}{120}y^2 - 12$

b. $\frac{x^2}{729} + \frac{y^2}{405} = 1$ **c.** $\frac{x^2}{116.64} - \frac{y^2}{207.36} = 1$

Equation Solving in Ancient Civilizations, pages 15–16

1. Since $x = \frac{2}{3}$ is a root of $9x^3 + 3x^2 - 4 = 0$, $3x - 2$ is a factor of $9x^3 + 3x^2 - 4$. Dividing $9x^3 + 3x^2 - 4$ by $3x - 2$ gives $3x^2 + 3x + 2$. The quadratic formula shows that the roots of $3x^2 + 3x + 2 = 0$ are imaginary. Thus, $x = \frac{2}{3}$ is the only real root of $9x^3 + 3x^2 - 4 = 0$.   **2.** This method is only useful in solving cubic equations of the form $ax^3 + bx^2 = c$ where k is a constant such that kax^3 is a perfect cube and kbx^2 is a perfect square.

3. $2x^3 + x^2 = 20$; multiply both sides by 4; $8x^3 + 4x^2 = 80$; let $n = 2x$; $n^3 + n^2 = 80$; $n = 4$; $2x = 4$; $x = 2$.

4. a. $x^3 + 4x = 12$; $x^4 + 4x^2 = 12x$; $x^4 = 12x - 4x^2$; $\frac{x^4}{4} = 3x - x^2$; $\frac{x^2}{2} = \pm\sqrt{x(3 - x)}$ **b.** Let $y = \pm\sqrt{x(3 - x)}$; then $y^2 = x(3 - x)$, and $\frac{x^2}{2} = y$ or $x^2 = 2y$.

5. $y^2 = x(3 - x)$; $y^2 = 3x - x^2$; $x^2 - 3x + y^2 = 0$; $x^2 - 3x + \frac{9}{4} + y^2 = \frac{9}{4}$; $\left(x - \frac{3}{2}\right)^2 + y^2 = \frac{9}{4}$; circle with center $\left(\frac{3}{2}, 0\right)$ and radius $\frac{3}{2}$.

6. a.

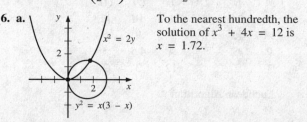

To the nearest hundredth, the solution of $x^3 + 4x = 12$ is $x = 1.72$.

b. Multiplying both sides of $x^3 + 4x = 12$ by x produced the extraneous root $x = 0$.   **7.** $x = 4$ **8. a.** $x = \pm240$ or $x = \pm840$ **b.** $x = \pm3$

Working with Radians, pages 17–18

1. $\frac{x}{360} \cdot 2\pi(1) = \frac{\pi x}{180}$ **2.** Answers may vary. For example, the triangle determined by your eye and the ends of the strip is almost equilateral, so the angle that your eye makes with the ends of the strip is about 60°, which is approximately 1 radian.

3. a.   **b.**

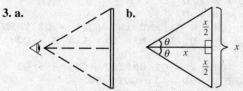

Since the distance to the strip is equal to the length of the strip, we have the diagram at the right above. Since $\tan\theta = \frac{\frac{x}{2}}{x} = \frac{1}{2}$, $\theta \approx 0.46$ (radians) and $2\theta \approx 0.93$. Thus, our approximation of 1 radian is too small.   **4.** Answers will vary. For example, if a bookcase has the same apparent size as the radian strip when you are standing 5 ft away from the bookcase, then the bookcase is about 5 ft tall.

ADVANCED MATHEMATICS
Activities Book

5. In the diagram,

$\triangle ESP \sim \triangle EOT$, so

$\frac{SP}{OT} = \frac{x}{y}$. Since $SP = x$ by

construction, $OT = y$. In
other words, the size of the
object equals the distance to
the object.

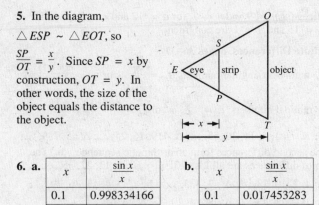

6. a.

x	$\frac{\sin x}{x}$
0.1	0.998334166
0.01	0.999983333
0.001	0.999999833

b.

x	$\frac{\sin x}{x}$
0.1	0.017453283
0.01	0.017453292
0.001	0.017453292

c. In degree mode, the calculator interprets the x in the numerator of $\frac{\sin x}{x}$ as an angular measure, but it interprets the x in the denominator as a linear measure. As Ex. 1 shows, if a central angle of a unit circle has a measure of x degrees, then it intercepts an arc that is $\frac{\pi x}{180}$ units long, not x units long. Thus, as the value of x (measured in degrees) approaches 0, the value of $\frac{\sin x}{\frac{\pi x}{180}}$ would approach 1, but the value of $\frac{\sin x}{x}$ would not.

d. Since $\frac{\sin x}{x} = \frac{\pi}{180} \cdot \frac{\sin x}{\frac{\pi x}{180}}$, the value of $\frac{\sin x}{x}$ approaches

$\frac{\pi}{180} \cdot 1 = \frac{\pi}{180}$ as the value of x (measured in degrees) approaches 0.

Making Waves, pages 19–20

1. The cut edge of the paper resembles a sine wave.   **2.** The cut edge of the paper again resembles a sine wave. The smaller diameter produces a sine wave with a smaller period, that is, with greater frequency.   **3.** Decreasing the angle measure from 45° to 30° decreases the amplitude of the sine wave.   **4.** Changing the diameter of the candle affects the frequency of the sine wave; changing the angle of the cut affects the amplitude of the sine wave.
5. The cut edge resembles a "sawtooth":

There are two ways to cut the
paper, as shown at the right.
6. The pencil traces out a sine wave.   **7.** Pulling the paper faster increases the frequency (the number of cycles per sheet of paper).   **8.** Pull the paper at the same rate, but move the pencil back and forth more quickly.   **9.** Change the length of the slit in the cardboard.

Circles and Spheres in Architecture, pages 21–22

1. Answers may vary. Examples: climate, geological stability, limitations created by available building materials. Circular shapes allow maximum area for given perimeter.   **2. a.** The volume of the dome is about 2094 m³; the volume of the cube is about 1409 m³. A sphere having the same surface area as the hemisphere or the cube would enclose greater volume.

b. The area of the dome's floor is about 314 m²; the area of the cube's floor is about 247 m². The dome has more floor space.   **3.** C and C' have the same perimeter and C' encloses an area greater than that enclosed by C. This contradicts the assumption that C is the curve with perimeter P that encloses maximum area.   **4.** If the two areas are not equal, reflect the region of greater area in $\overline{XY}$. The new curve has perimeter P and encloses a greater area than C does. This produces the same contradiction as in Ex. 3.   **5. a.** In the given triangles, $OX' = OX$ and $OY' = OY$. Area of $\triangle X'OY' =$

$\frac{1}{2} \cdot OX' \cdot OY' \cdot \sin 90° > \frac{1}{2} \cdot OX \cdot OY \cdot \sin \angle XOY =$

area of $\triangle XOY$. Thus, the area enclosed by $\overset{\frown}{X'OY'}$ and $\overline{X'Y'}$ is

greater than the area enclosed by $\overset{\frown}{XOY}$ and $\overline{XY}$. But this

contradicts the assumption that $\overset{\frown}{XOY}$ and $\overline{XY}$ enclose a

region of maximum area.   **b.** If, for every point O on $\overset{\frown}{XOY}$, $\angle XOY$ is a right angle, then O is a vertex of a right triangle

with hypotenuse $\overline{XY}$. Let M be the midpoint of $\overline{XY}$. M is equidistant from O, X, and Y. That is, for every O on $\overset{\frown}{XOY}$,

$OM = \frac{1}{2}XY$. $\overset{\frown}{XOY}$ is, by definition, a semicircle. Therefore,

C is a circle with center M and radius $\frac{1}{2}XY$.   **6.** Such a shape permits maximum volume of storage space for a given surface area, which allows the most economical use of construction materials.   **7. a.** A sphere or hemisphere; for a given volume, the figure with minimum surface area is a sphere.   **b.** Since the shape with minimum surface area for a given volume is a sphere, a dome-shaped building would have less heat loss than any other building of equal volume.

Sums of Sine Waves, pages 24–25

1. a. 2, 3, 6   **b.** $1, \frac{4}{3}, 4$ **c.** $\pi, \frac{2\pi}{3}, 2\pi$ **c.** The period of $h(x) = f(x) + g(x)$ is the least common multiple of the periods of f and g.   **3. a.** 12, 5, 13   **b.** 0.7, 2.4, 2.5   **c.** 8, 6, 10
4. (amp. of h)² = (amp. of f)² + (amp. of g)²
5. a. $-5 = 13 \cos C$ and $12 = -13 \sin C$; $C \approx 4.32$; $h(x) = 13 \sin (x - 4.32)$ **b.** $-2.4 = 2.5 \cos C$ and $-0.7 = -2.5 \sin C$; $C \approx 2.86$; $h(x) = 2.5 \sin (x - 2.86)$
c. $8 = 10 \cos 2C$ and $-6 = -10 \sin 2C$; $2C \approx 0.64$; $C \approx 0.32$; $h(x) = 10 \sin 2(x - 0.32)$ **6.** $h(x) = A_1 \sin x + A_2 \cos x = A_3 \sin (x - C) = A_3(\sin x \cos C - \cos x \sin C) = (A_3 \cos C) \sin x + (-A_3 \sin C) \cos x$; $A_1 = A_3 \cos C$ and $A_2 = -A_3 \sin C$; $\sqrt{(A_1)^2 + (A_2)^2} = \sqrt{(A_3 \cos C)^2 + (-A_3 \sin C)^2} = \sqrt{(A_3)^2(\cos^2 C + \sin^2 C)} = \sqrt{(A_3)^2 \cdot 1} = A_3$

History of Trigonometry, pages 26–27

1. a. Seqt is proportional to the reciprocal of slope.

b. $\text{seqt} = \frac{\text{run}}{\text{rise}} = \frac{BC \text{ hands}}{AB \text{ cubits}} = \frac{BC \text{ hands}}{7 \, AB \text{ hands}} = \frac{\cot \theta}{7}$

c. $\frac{180 \text{ cubits}}{250 \text{ cubits}} = \frac{7 \cdot 180 \text{ hands}}{250 \text{ cubits}} = 5\frac{1}{25}$ hands per cubit

2. Answers will vary. A vertical stick, called a "gnomon," casts a shadow, $\overline{PN}$. The length of the shadow depends on the time of the year and the time of day. Since the length GN is constant, the length PN depends on the measure of $\angle P$. Thus, the sundial uses the concept of tangent in its construction.

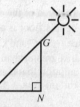

3. Answers will vary. Hipparchus wrote 12 books on the computation of chords of circles. The tables contained in these books are thought to be the first trigonometric tables. The tables were used by Hipparchus in his work on astronomy.

4. $84 + \dfrac{51}{60} + \dfrac{10}{60^2} \approx 84.8528$; $60\sqrt{2} \approx 84.8528$ **5.** 60^{p}

6. $\sin \alpha = \dfrac{\frac{1}{2}AB}{r} = \dfrac{AB}{2(60)} = \dfrac{\mathrm{cd}\ 2\alpha}{120}$ **7.** Answers will vary.

a. Aryabhata developed the concept of the trigonometric functions of an angle, including tables of half-chords.
b. François Viète developed methods for solving plane and spherical triangles with the use of all six trigonometric functions.

Spirals, pages 28–29
1. a spiral **2.** The second curve is wider than the first. **3.** A tighter spiral is formed. **4.** A faster turntable speed produces a tighter spiral. **5.** As you pull the pen toward you from the center of rotation, you must also move the pen in the direction of rotation. Creating a straight line in this way is difficult to do. **6.** Do not move the pen as the turntable rotates. **7. a.** an arc of a spiral **b.** 2 points that are equidistant from the center of rotation **8.** Answers will vary.

Friction, page 30
1. Since $\angle A \cong \angle A$ and $\angle AED$ and $\angle ACB$ are both right angles, $\triangle ADE \sim \triangle ABC$ by AA Similarity.

2. $\dfrac{|\mathbf{f_s}|}{\sqrt{|\mathbf{w}|^2 - |\mathbf{f_s}|^2}} = \dfrac{y}{x}$; $\dfrac{|\mathbf{f_s}|^2}{|\mathbf{w}|^2 - |\mathbf{f_s}|^2} = \dfrac{y^2}{x^2}$;

$|\mathbf{f_s}|^2 x^2 = |\mathbf{w}|^2 y^2 - |\mathbf{f_s}|^2 y^2$; $|\mathbf{f_s}|^2 (x^2 + y^2) = |\mathbf{w}|^2 y^2$;

$|\mathbf{f_s}|^2 = \dfrac{y^2 |\mathbf{w}|}{x^2 + y^2}$; $|\mathbf{f_s}| = \dfrac{y|\mathbf{w}|}{\sqrt{x^2 + y^2}}$ **3.** Answers will vary.

A Journey into Four-Dimensional Space, pages 31–35
1.

	Point	Segment	Square	Cube	Hypercube
Vertices	1	2	4	8	16
Edges	—	1	4	12	32
Faces	—	—	1	6	24
Cubes	—	—	—	1	8

2. The slices are equilateral triangles for $n = 1, 2, 3, 4, 8, 9, 10, 11$. The slices are hexagons (with 3 short congruent sides and 3 long congruent sides that alternate) for $n = 5, 7$. The slice is a regular hexagon for $n = 6$. **3.** The slices are congruent for each pair $n = k$ and $n = 12 - k$ where $k = 1, 2, 3, 4, 5$. **4.** The slices are regular tetrahedrons for $n = 1, 2, 3, 4$. The slices are octahedrons (formed by "cutting off" the corners of tetrahedrons) for $n = 5, 6, 7$. The slice is a regular octahedron for $n = 8$. **5.** The slices are congruent pairwise ($n = k$ and $n = 16 - k$ for $k = 1, 2, \ldots, 7$). In particular, the slices for $n = 9$ and $n = 7$, for $n = 12$ and $n = 5$, and for $n = 15$ and $n = 1$ are congruent.

Finite Differences, pages 36–37
1. neither; triangular numbers: $t_n = \displaystyle\sum_{k=1}^{n} k$ or $t_n = \dfrac{n(n+1)}{2}$;

pyramidal numbers: $t_n = \displaystyle\sum_{k=1}^{n} k^2$ or $t_n = \dfrac{n(n+1)(2n+1)}{6}$

2. a. t_n: 1, 5, 14, 30, 55, …; Δ: 4, 9, 16, 25, …; Δ^2: 5, 7, 9, …; the second differences form an arithmetic sequence **b.** The third differences are all 2's. **3. a.** t_n: 1, 5, 12, 22, 35, …; Δ: 4, 7, 10, 13, …; Δ^2: 3, 3, 3, … **b.** t_n: 3, 4, 13, 36, 79, …; Δ: 1, 9, 23, 43, …; Δ^2: 8, 14, 20, …; Δ^3: 6, 6, … **c.** t_n: −4, 0, 10, 26, 48, …; Δ: 4, 10, 16, 22, …; Δ^2: 6, 6, 6, … **4.** t_n: $a + b + c, 4a + 2b + c, 9a + 3b + c$, $16a + 4b + c, 25a + 5b + c, \ldots$; Δ: $3a + b, 5a + b, 7a + b, 9a + b, \ldots$; Δ^2: $2a, 2a, 2a, \ldots$ **5.** $t_{25} = 325$ **6. a.** t_n: $a + b + c + d, 8a + 4b + 2c + d$, $27a + 9b + 3c + d, 64a + 16b + 4c + d$, $125a + 25b + 5c + d, \ldots$; Δ: $7a + 3b + c, 19a + 5b + c$, $37a + 7b + c, 61a + 9b + c, \ldots$; Δ^2: $12a + 2b, 18a + 2b$, $24a + 2b, \ldots$; Δ^3: $6a, 6a, \ldots$ **b.** $a = \dfrac{1}{3}$; $b = \dfrac{1}{2}$; $c = \dfrac{1}{6}$; $d = 0$; $t_n = \dfrac{2n^3 + 3n^2 + n}{6} = \dfrac{n(n+1)(2n+1)}{6}$

7. a. $t_n = \dfrac{n(3n-1)}{2}$ **b.** $t_n = n^3 - 2n^2 + 4$ **c.** $t_n = 3n^2 - 5n - 2$ **8. a.** t_n: 27, 91, 216, 432, 775, 1287, …; Δ: 64, 125, 216, 343, 512, …; Δ^2: 61, 91, 127, 169, …; Δ^3: 30, 36, 42, …; Δ^4: 6, 6, … **b.** 4

An Introduction to Cryptology, pages 38–40
1. MGEQICMWE. CMGSRUYIVIHB
2. BEWARE THE IDES.
3.

Plain text	A	B	C	D	E	F	G	H	I	J	K	L
Value	0	1	2	3	4	5	6	7	8	9	10	11
Encoded value	0	2	4	6	8	10	12	14	16	18	20	22
Cipher text	A	C	E	G	I	K	M	O	Q	S	U	W

M	N	O	P	Q	R	S	T	U	V	W	X	Y	Z	.	,	?
12	13	14	15	16	17	18	19	20	21	22	23	24	25	26	27	28
24	26	28	1	3	5	7	9	11	13	15	17	19	21	23	25	27
Y	.	?	B	D	F	H	J	L	N	P	R	T	V	X	Z	,

4. a.

Plain text	A	B	C	D	E	F	G	H	I	J
Value	0	1	2	3	4	5	6	7	8	9
Encoded value	0	2	4	6	8	10	12	14	16	18
Cipher text	A	C	E	G	I	K	M	O	Q	S

K	L	M	N	O	P	Q	R	S	T	U	V	W	X	Y	Z
10	11	12	13	14	15	16	17	18	19	20	21	22	23	24	25
20	22	24	0	2	4	6	8	10	12	14	16	18	20	22	24
U	W	Y	A	C	E	G	I	K	M	O	Q	S	U	W	Y

b. The code is not one-to-one; each letter in the cipher text is associated with two letters in plain text; half the possible cipher letters aren't used.

ADVANCED MATHEMATICS
Activities Book

c.

Plain text	A	B	C	D	E	F	G	H	I	J
Value	0	1	2	3	4	5	6	7	8	9
Encoded value	0	3	6	9	12	15	18	21	24	1
Cipher text	A	D	G	J	M	P	S	V	Y	B

K	L	M	N	O	P	Q	R	S	T	U	V	W	X	Y	Z
10	11	12	13	14	15	16	17	18	19	20	21	22	23	24	25
4	7	10	13	16	19	22	25	2	5	8	11	14	17	20	23
E	H	K	N	Q	T	W	Z	C	F	I	L	O	R	U	X

This code is one-to-one, so the problem has been eliminated.
d. If the multiplier and the modulus have a common factor other than 1, the code is not one-to-one. If the multiplier and the modulus are relatively prime, then the code is one-to-one and thus appropriate. **5.** To encode each letter from A to Z, add 5 to the opposite of each character value. If the sum is negative, add 26 to the sum to obtain the encoded value.
6. Multiply the encoded value by 15; if the product is greater than 28, subtract 29 as many times as necessary to produce a number from 0 to 28, inclusive. That number is the plain-text value, which can be used to write the associated plain-text character. **7.** Answers will vary. For example, "GOOD DAY, MATE" is encoded as "UBCGAIZESNWV".

8. $\begin{bmatrix} 24 & 6 \\ 18 & 12 \end{bmatrix} \begin{bmatrix} 22 & 5 \\ 6 & 0 \end{bmatrix} = \begin{bmatrix} 564 & 120 \\ 468 & 90 \end{bmatrix} \rightarrow$

$\begin{bmatrix} 13 & 4 \\ 4 & 3 \end{bmatrix} \rightarrow \begin{bmatrix} N & E \\ E & D \end{bmatrix}$;

$\begin{bmatrix} 24 & 6 \\ 18 & 12 \end{bmatrix} \begin{bmatrix} 3 & 22 \\ 23 & 19 \end{bmatrix} = \begin{bmatrix} 210 & 642 \\ 330 & 624 \end{bmatrix} \rightarrow$

$\begin{bmatrix} 7 & 4 \\ 11 & 15 \end{bmatrix} \rightarrow \begin{bmatrix} H & E \\ L & P \end{bmatrix}$

9. $\begin{bmatrix} 3 & -4 \\ 5 & -2 \end{bmatrix}^{-1} = 27 \begin{bmatrix} -2 & 4 \\ -5 & 3 \end{bmatrix} =$

$\begin{bmatrix} -54 & 108 \\ -135 & 81 \end{bmatrix} \rightarrow \begin{bmatrix} 4 & 21 \\ 10 & 23 \end{bmatrix}$

Derangements: Nothing in Its Proper Place, pages 41–43
1. BCA, CAB **2.** 2143, 2341, 2413, 3142, 3412, 3421, 4123, 4312, 4321 **3. a.** $n(P_1 \cup P_2 \cup P_3 \cup P_4) = [n(P_1) + n(P_2) + n(P_3) + n(P_4)] - [n(P_1 \cap P_2) + n(P_1 \cap P_3) + n(P_1 \cap P_4) + n(P_2 \cap P_3) + n(P_2 \cap P_4) + n(P_3 \cap P_4)] + [n(P_1 \cap P_2 \cap P_3) + n(P_1 \cap P_2 \cap P_4) + n(P_1 \cap P_3 \cap P_4) + n(P_2 \cap P_3 \cap P_4)] - [n(P_1 \cap P_2 \cap P_3 \cap P_4)] = [6 + 6 + 6 + 6] - [2 + 2 + 2 + 2 + 2 + 2] + [1 + 1 + 1 + 1] - 1 = 24 - 12 + 4 - 1 = 15$
b. $n(\text{derangements}) = 4! - 15 = 24 - 15 = 9$; agrees with answer in Exercise 2 **4. a.** In each addend, two of the digits are fixed in position, and the remaining 2 positions can be filled in 2! ways. Thus, $n(P_1 \cap P_2) + n(P_1 \cap P_3) + n(P_1 \cap P_4) + n(P_2 \cap P_3) + n(P_2 \cap P_4) + n(P_3 \cap P_4) = 2! + 2! + 2! + 2! + 2! + 2! = {}_4C_2 \cdot 2!$
b. ${}_4C_3 \cdot 1!$; ${}_4C_4 \cdot 0!$ **c.** $n(\text{derangements}) = 4! - [{}_4C_1 \cdot 3! - {}_4C_2 \cdot 2! + {}_4C_3 \cdot 1! - {}_4C_4 \cdot 0!] = 4! - {}_4C_1 \cdot 3! + {}_4C_2 \cdot 2! - {}_4C_3 \cdot 1! + {}_4C_4 \cdot 0!$

5. 44 **6.** $6! \left[1 - \frac{1}{1!} + \frac{1}{2!} - \frac{1}{3!} + \frac{1}{4!} - \frac{1}{5!} + \frac{1}{6!} \right] = 265$

7. a. $d_7 = 7! \left[1 - \frac{1}{1!} + \frac{1}{2!} - \frac{1}{3!} + \frac{1}{4!} - \frac{1}{5!} + \frac{1}{6!} - \frac{1}{7!} \right] = 1854$ **b.** $d_7 = 7 \cdot d_6 + (-1)^7 = 7(265) - 1 = 1854$

8. $d_n = \begin{cases} 0 & \text{if } n = 1 \\ 1 & \text{if } n = 2 \\ (n-1)[d_{n-1} + d_{n-2}] & \text{if } n > 2 \end{cases}$

9. a.
```
10 LET D = 0
20 INPUT "NUMBER OF OBJECTS:   ";N
30 IF N = 1 THEN GOTO 80
40 FOR I = 2 TO N
50 IF I/2 = INT(I/2) THEN LET D = I * D + 1
60 IF I/2 <> INT(I/2) THEN LET D = I * D - 1
70 NEXT I
80 PRINT "NUMBER OF DERANGEMENTS:   ";D
90 END
```
b. Running the program with $N = 26$ gives $D \approx 1.5 \times 10^{26}$.

Assessing Risk, pages 44–45
1. Answers may vary. **a.** If you don't mind getting wet, the risk is reasonable. **b.** A 10% chance of not getting home safely is unacceptable in the given circumstances.
2. Answers may vary. One study of risk-taking found that people tend to avoid risk when seeking gains, but choose risk to avoid losses. **3.** Answers may vary. Information from the National Safety Council indicates that for 1991 an ordering of major forms of transportation in the U.S., from most safe to least safe, was: buses, airplanes, trains, and automobiles.
4. a. $\approx 5.15 \times 10^8 \text{ km}^2$; $\approx 5.15 \times 10^{14} \text{ m}^2$
b. $\approx 3.9 \times 10^{-15}$ **c.** The probability of someone being hit was extremely small, even if 10 or 100 refrigerator-sized pieces fell to Earth. **5.** Answers will vary. Extensive media exposure probably makes people perceive a much greater risk than actually exists. **6. a.** 0.00000012; the increased probability of a local individual developing cancer if the plant is operated **b.** With a probability of 0.2, about 200,000 of every 1,000,000 people could be expected to develop cancer. The increase caused by the recycling plant is insignificant.
c. Answers may vary. Since the increased risk is so slight, it seems unreasonable to have stopped construction of the plant.
d. Answers will vary. Examples: Is the computer study a reliable simulation? Can the recycling plant be modified to reduce or eliminate the increase in the cancer rate?
7. Answers will vary. Examples that might be considered: playing sports, driving a car, working at a construction site.

Factorial Designs, pages 46–47
1.

		Viewpoint			Row means
		liberal	moderate	conservative	
Opinion	yes	3.00	3.20	3.06	3.09
	no	3.26	3.36	3.24	3.29
Column means		3.13	3.28	3.15	

2. Yes; people who think that recycling is worth the cost and effort had a lower average amount of trash. Because the comparison is based on opinion *regardless of viewpoint*, the comparison is a measure of the main effect of opinion.

ADVANCED MATHEMATICS
Activities Book

3. Yes, but not as great an effect as opinion does. Those with liberal or conservative viewpoints produce less trash than those with moderate viewpoints.

4. a.

		Viewpoint		
		liberal	moderate	conservative
Opinion	yes	3.00	3.20	3.06
	no	3.26	3.36	3.24
Column means		−0.26	−0.16	−0.18

b. Yes; the difference in means for liberals is greater (in absolute value) than that for either moderates or conservatives.
5. a. If there is no interaction, then the differences between people of different opinions (measured by the distances between vertically-aligned pairs of points on the graph) would not depend on the viewpoint; that is, the distances would not vary from one viewpoint to another. Thus, the distance remains constant and the broken-line graphs are parallel when there is no interaction. Clearly, the distances *will* vary if there is an interaction.

b.

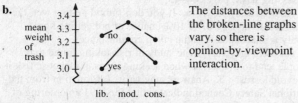

The distances between the broken-line graphs vary, so there is opinion-by-viewpoint interaction.

6. Answers will vary.

Comparing Residuals, pages 48–50
1. $y_i < f(x_i)$, so $e_i = y_i - f(x_i) < 0$.   **2. a.** Residuals: −11.6, 3.7, 0.1, 14.4, 1.9, −2.1, −2.7, 5.2, −1.8, −7.2; as long as some of the data points are above the line and some are below it, some of the residuals will be positive and some will be negative.   **b.** If some residuals are positive and some are negative, adding them together to compute the mean results in residuals "canceling out" each other. Thus, the mean of the residuals may be close to 0 even if the data points are far from the line.   **3.** MSE ≈ 45.3; MSE would be considered high.
4. a. Answers may vary slightly. $f(x) = 33.46x - 2420.4$; MSE ≈ 41.76   **b.** The MSE would be considered low.
5. The y-values in Ex. 4 are much larger than those in Ex. 3; when expressed as percentages of these y-values, the residuals are therefore much smaller in Ex. 4 than in Ex. 3 (which explains why a line fits the data better in Ex. 4 than in Ex. 3). This shows that you cannot compare MSE's when fitting a line (or any other curve) to different sets of data.   **6. a.** Answers may vary slightly. $f(x) = (0.0390)1.1155^x$; MSE ≈ 181.9
b. The line *seems* to give a better fit than the exponential curve.   **7.** The same set of data is used in computing the MSE's for the line and the exponential curve. Since the line's MSE is smaller, the line provides a better fit.   **8. a.** Answers may vary slightly. $f(x) = (2.068 \times 10^{-15})x^{8.972}$;   MSE ≈ 135.5   **b.** Of the three MSE's, the line's MSE is smallest. Therefore, the line provides the best fit.

Another Look at Julia Sets, pages 51–52
1. The set of points is a circle of radius 1.   **2.** The shapes of the two Julia sets are the same, but the Julia set produced by the inverse iteration method does not show as complete a border as that of the filled-in Julia set.

3. a. inside   **b.** i   **c.** both   **4. a.** on the border   **b.** ii   **c.** point symmetry   **5. a.** outside   **b.** iv   **c.** point symmetry   **6. a.** outside   **b.** iii   **c.** point symmetry   **7. a.** inside   **b.** ii   **c.** both   **8. a.** outside   **b.** iv   **c.** point symmetry   **9.** They are all mostly connected curves that enclose one or more regions.   **10.** Either they are disconnected clumps of points or they are mostly connected lines that do not enclose regions.   **11.** The sets are reflections of each other with respect to a horizontal line.   **12.** for a complex constant c on the real axis

Position, Velocity, and Acceleration, pages 53–54
1. a. Divide the distance covered, 100 mi, by the travel time, 2 h; speed = 50 mi/h.   **b.** The slope of the line would be smaller.   **2.** Graphs may vary. An example is given below.

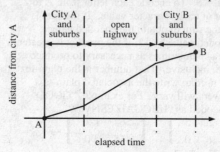

3. a. If you count the bulleted points on the graph from left to right (so that the origin is "point 1"), then A is the fifth point, B is the third point, and C is the seventh point.   **b.** When the teacher is on the highway; the graph is steepest during that period of time.   **c.** When the teacher is stopped behind the school bus; the graph is horizontal during that period of time.

4. Sketches may vary. An example is shown at the right.

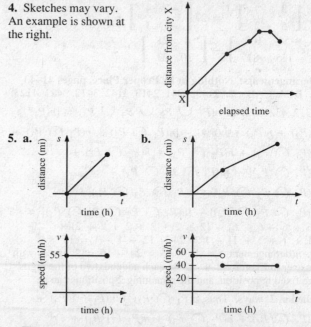

5. a.   **b.**

c. The speed-versus-time graph will become continuous, with the two horizontal pieces joined by a smooth curve of gradually decreasing steepness. On the distance-versus-time graph, the "corner" will become rounded and smooth.

ADVANCED MATHEMATICS
Activities Book